Copyright © 2025 John Cunningham
All rights reserved

Contents

ABOUT ME 4
INTRODUCTION 5
CHAPTER 1: IS A CAREER IN B2B SALES RIGHT FOR YOU? 7
CHAPTER 2: WHAT DOES IT TAKE TO BE SUCCESSFUL IN B2B SALES? 11
CHAPTER 3: BUILDING YOUR PERSONAL BRAND 15
CHAPTER 4: UNDERSTANDING THE B2B SALES CYCLE 21
CHAPTER 5: THE DECISION-MAKING PROCESS 28
CHAPTER 6: THE BASIS OF DECISION 41
CHAPTER 7: IDENTIFYING YOUR IDEAL CUSTOMER TARGET MARKET PROFILE 50
CHAPTER 8: PROSPECTING 57
CHAPTER 9: PREPARING FOR CUSTOMER MEETINGS 75
CHAPTER 10: QUALIFICATION, QUALIFICATION, QUALIFICATION 84
CHAPTER 11: ASKING THE RIGHT QUESTIONS 97
CHAPTER 12: ACTIVE LISTENING AND READING NON-VERBAL CLUES 106
CHAPTER 13: UNDERSTANDING CUSTOMER PERSONALITY TYPES 114
CHAPTER 14: WRITING WINNING SALES PROPOSALS 121
CHAPTER 15: PRESENTING YOUR PROPOSAL 134
CHAPTER 16: OBJECTION HANDLING: TURNING CHALLENGES INTO OPPORTUNITIES 145
CHAPTER 17: NEGOTIATION 159
CHAPTER 18: CLOSING 179
CHAPTER 19: UPSELLING AND CROSS-SELLING 192
CHAPTER 20: DEVELOPING YOUR SKILL SET 197
CHAPTER 21: PULLING IT ALL TOGETHER: THE BEST VERSION OF YOU 200

For Kathy, who made me a better person

About me

I began my professional career as a helicopter controller in Britain's Royal Navy and progressed with roles at Crown Lift Trucks, Case Communications, Pace Micro and Telewest, through to leadership of the largest Virgin Group B2B sales operation in the world at Virgin Media Business.

I'm not really sure how I got from being a member of the armed forces to being a sales director, though I suspect that like a lot of people, "sales" is somewhere I ended up, rather than being the destination I had in mind when I set off.

In 2010, I decided to pull the ripcord on the parachute of corporate life and founded johnpc ltd, the objective being to create a company through which I could share my experience (both good and not so good) and expertise with a wider audience on an independent basis.

This is a journey which has been profitable and rewarding in equal measure, giving me an opportunity to learn a lot about myself and how I can become better at what I do.

The motivation for writing the book came after I was unfortunately diagnosed with oropharyngeal cancer in 2021, which meant that by the end of 2024 I was forced to curtail my johnpc ltd activities. I decided to put what I know (at least what I can remember) down in print.

I hope you enjoy the book.

Publisher's note

John Cunningham died in February 2025, after putting the finishing touches to this book. He was a much-admired figure in the business community, and his vast experience – more than 40 years in B2B sales – resonates in every chapter. His knowledge is so valuable that Q5, a consultancy that he worked with, is publishing it posthumously.

John was a devoted husband of 45 years to Kathy, a proud father to Neil and Mark, and a doting grandad to Lilly and Chloe. He is much missed.

Introduction

A career in business-to-business (B2B) sales for me has been a journey of learning, fun, high stakes and considerable rewards. It's taught me that at its core lies a fundamental truth: your results determine your future. It's all about winning.

Achieving your targets consistently opens doors to bigger opportunities, career advancements, recognition and the satisfaction of a job well done. Conversely, falling short can make sales an unforgiving environment, where there are no silver or bronze medals, only winners and others left to try again.

The title of this book, **"Your Numbers Shall Set You Free,"** was a personal mantra that I would constantly articulate to anyone who would listen. It's a call to action and a guiding principle. Your performance, measured in tangible results, is not just a metric; it's your pathway to growth and success in a very competitive field.

However, over the years I've learnt that the route to long-term sustainable success in B2B sales demands a balance between art and science.

- **The art**: building meaningful relationships, earning trust, building credibility and connecting with clients on a personal level
- **The science**: implementing structured processes, leveraging data, and executing strategies with precision.

These two elements are inextricably linked. Mastery of the art without the science leads to inconsistency, while science without art creates a mechanical, impersonal approach. It's only by integrating both that sales people can thrive, be successful (and set themselves free).

The purpose of this book

The primary purpose of this book is to offer you a thorough understanding of the B2B sales cycle and to equip you with the tools needed to excel in every stage of the process. From conducting successful customer meetings to mastering negotiations, I hope to cover all aspects of B2B sales and delve into a number of crucial topics including effective questioning and understanding customer personality types and closing the sale.

How to use this book

I've structured the book to be a flexible resource, allowing you to dip into specific sections as needed rather than reading it cover to cover. Whether you're preparing for a customer meeting, looking for new ways to engage with customers or seeking to develop your personal brand, you will find relevant and actionable information in each chapter.

By integrating models, techniques and best practices from my own personal experiences, I hope to enhance your skills and confidence in every sales interaction. Real-life scenarios, models and examples are included to illustrate how these concepts are applied in practical situations.

As you navigate through the book, you will encounter various tools and strategies designed to help you achieve success in the competitive B2B marketplace. Use this book as a companion and reference guide to sharpen your sales acumen and drive your success.

Who will benefit from reading this book?

My hope is that the book acts as a guide that serves as your trusted sales companion, whether you are an experienced sales person seeking to refine your approach or a newcomer taking the first steps in your sales career.

It goes without saying (I hope) that the two biggest contributors to a successful sale career both come from you. They are a commitment to learn and try new things and the hard work to prepare to be the best version of yourself at all times. The timeless adage of '*practice makes perfect"* resonates in this world as highly as any other high stakes profession.

Thank you for choosing this book as your guide. I'm excited to share what I've learned and I hope I can help you achieve a B2B sales career that delivers as much to you as mine has to me.

Chapter 1: Is a career in B2B sales right for you?

"The only way to do great work is to love what you do." - Steve Jobs.

Choosing a career as a B2B salesperson isn't just a job choice. It's a commitment to a dynamic, multifaceted and potentially rewarding career journey. The motivations behind wanting to be a B2B salesperson are diverse, ranging from financial aspirations to a love for problem-solving and relationship-building. In this chapter, I'll delve into the upsides and downsides of a B2B sales career, concluding with an overview of three characteristics of the profile best suited and not suited to achieving long-term sustainable success.

Firstly, let's explore the potential upsides of a career in B2B sales.

1. No two days are the same

One of the most exciting aspects of a career in B2B sales for me is the variety. No two days are the same, which keeps the job dynamic and engaging. Each day presents new challenges, opportunities, and interactions. This variety ensures that you're constantly learning and adapting.

2. Financial rewards

Another significant (and obvious) attraction of B2B sales is the potential for substantial financial rewards. You will often operate on commission and bonus structures, directly tying earnings to their performance. Successfully closed deals and exceeded targets translate into higher income, providing a tangible reward for your efforts.

3. Rewarding relationships

In B2B sales, relationships matter deeply. If you thrive on dynamic and rewarding interactions, it's a career that provides the opportunity to build connections that go beyond transactional exchanges. The satisfaction derived from cultivating and nurturing long-term partnerships (and friends) is a driving force for many in B2B sales.

4. Problem-solving

B2B salespeople find motivation in solving problems. Understanding the challenges faced by customers and presenting solutions that genuinely address them is not just a transaction, but a strategic collaboration that can have a lasting impact on both parties.

5. Continuous learning and adaptation

The ever-evolving nature of B2B sales demands that you engage in continuous learning and adaptation. If you relish staying informed about your own and your competitors' products and services, industry trends, market dynamics, and innovative sales strategies; it's a stimulating environment that fosters intellectual growth and professional development.

6. Versatility and transferable skills

The ability to communicate effectively, negotiate and build relationships are skills that transcend industries. This versatility not only enhances success in the sales field, it also makes you well-equipped for diverse roles and sectors. In short, good salespeople with transferable skills are (and always will be) in demand.

Now, let's look at the potential downsides of a career in B2B sales.

1. Rejection and resilience

One of the primary downsides of a career in B2B sales is the inevitable encounter with rejection. Salespeople face the challenge of handling rejection gracefully, maintaining confidence and persevering in the face of setbacks. Developing personal resilience is crucial to navigate the emotional toll that rejection can take.

2. High-pressure environment

B2B sales is often characterised by high-pressure environments, particularly when dealing with ambitious targets or high-stakes deals. Meeting quotas and achieving sales goals requires a proactive and results-oriented mindset, which can cope with stress and pressure.

3. Long sales cycles

The patience and persistence required to navigate through extended decision-making processes and negotiations can be challenging. Successful sales people need to be adept at managing expectations and sustaining their efforts over prolonged periods.

4. Uncertain income

While the potential for high earnings exists, the income of a B2B salesperson can be variable and dependent on various factors, such as market conditions, economic fluctuations, and individual performance. This level of income uncertainty may not suit individuals who prefer stable and predictable income streams.

5. **Constant adaptation to market changes**

The dynamic nature of markets and industries means that B2B sales professionals must be adept at constantly adapting to changes, whether it's learning about new technologies, adjusting strategies or pivoting to address evolving customer demands. The need for continuous adaptation can be challenging for those not open to embracing change.

6. **Intensive workload and travel**

B2B sales roles can demand an intensive workload, particularly during peak periods or when pursuing high-value, complex opportunities. Travel may also be a significant aspect of the job, impacting work-life balance and requiring individuals to manage their time effectively.

From this, it follows that a career in B2B sales might suit some people but not others, depending on the individual's particular strengths, preferences, and aspirations.

B2B sales may suit

- **Ambitious individuals.** B2B sales can be highly rewarding for ambitious individuals who are motivated by the potential for financial success, recognition and career advancement. The results-driven nature of the field aligns with their aspirations for achievement.

- **Relationship builders.** Individuals who excel at building and nurturing relationships often find fulfilment in B2B sales. The ability to build rapport and make dynamic and rewarding connections suits their interpersonal skills and people-oriented approach.

- **Solution-oriented problem solvers.** Those who derive satisfaction from solving complex problems are well-suited for B2B sales. The opportunity to address client challenges in a strategic manner aligns with their problem-solving mindset.

- **Resilient and adaptable individuals.** Resilience and adaptability are essential traits for success in B2B sales. Individuals who can navigate rejection with resilience and embrace change with adaptability are better equipped to thrive in the face of challenges.

Conversely, B2B sales may not suit:

- **Those seeking predictable income.** For individuals who prioritise stability and predictable income, the uncertain nature of B2B sales earnings may pose a challenge. The variable income structure may not align with their financial needs.

- **Individuals averse to high-pressure environments.** B2B sales can be demanding, especially when working towards ambitious targets. Individuals who prefer a more relaxed and low-stakes environment may find the pressure challenging.

- **Individuals not inclined toward continuous learning.** The dynamic nature of B2B sales requires individuals to take personal responsibility for their professional and personal development. Those who are not inclined toward continuous learning may find it challenging to be successful in such an evolving landscape.

So is it right for you?

Choosing to be a B2B salesperson is a decision that demands a realistic assessment of your own strengths, preferences, and aspirations. The upsides of financial rewards, dynamic relationships and recognition make B2B sales an attractive career choice for many.

However, the downsides of rejection, high-pressure environments, uncertain income, combined with the pressure of constantly being judged by results, can make for a heavy load to carry.

For those with the right mindset, the journey is a rewarding one, offering not just financial success, but also the satisfaction of building meaningful relationships and contributing to the growth of organisations.

For others, the challenges may outweigh the rewards. It's a journey that demands self-awareness, tenacity, and a genuine passion for the art and the science of sales.

Chapter 2: What does it take to be successful in B2B sales?

"Find out what you like doing best and get someone to pay you for doing it." - Katharine Whitehorn.

The key to success is simple: be someone people want to buy from, and sell something people want to buy. There you go, the perfect formula for a successful career in B2B sales.

The key thing is that sales success is never solely determined by the products or services being sold. It also hinges on the abilities, qualities and mindset of the salesperson.

The B2B landscape is dynamic, marked by shifting trends, emerging technologies, energetic competitors and demanding customers. In this complex environment, certain characteristics stand out as the building blocks of a successful B2B salesperson; someone who not only closes deals but builds lasting relationships, navigates challenges with finesse, and consistently exceeds expectations.

During my career I've had the privilege to work with (and learn from) some very talented salespeople who have had long and rewarding careers. Based on this experience, I have collated 10 characteristics that I most often encountered in these outstanding individuals.

1. **Emotional Intelligence**

A successful B2B salesperson is not just a seller. They are a problem-solver. Emotional intelligence lies at the core of their interactions. Understanding the challenges and aspirations of customers and viewing the world through their eyes is an essential skill. The ability to empathise and understand enables them to tailor solutions that genuinely address the unique needs of each customer they encounter. In the process of selling, empathy becomes a bridge that connects you to the buyer, fostering trust and cultivating a sense of partnership, laying the foundation for long-term relationships beyond the immediate transaction.

2. **Adaptability and continuous learning**

Successful salespeople are adaptable, quick to pivot in response to shifts in market dynamics, technological advancements, competitor strategies and changes in customer behaviour. They are avid learners, staying abreast of industry trends, competitors' strategies, and emerging technologies. Adaptability is not just about surviving change but thriving in it.

Moreover, and most importantly they take personal responsibility for their own learning and development and don't rely on others to spoon-feed them.

3. Intellectual horsepower

Sometimes the sales process can be akin to a chess game, where each move requires careful consideration and foresight. Successful sales people possess intellectual horsepower, meaning they can quickly grasp and understand complex concepts and data, facilitating better decision-making and strategy formulation. They approach each opportunity as a unique puzzle, leveraging their problem-solving skills to tailor solutions that align with the client's goals. This attitude and mindset extends beyond individual transactions to encompass a broader understanding of market trends, competitive landscapes, and the overall direction of the industries in which they operate.

4. Effective communication

Communication is the cornerstone of successful B2B selling. Being adept at both verbal and written communication allows salespeople to articulate complex ideas to their customers in a clear and compelling manner. They listen actively to their clients, picking up on subtle cues and uncovering unspoken needs. Whether in a face-to-face meeting, a phone call, web meet or a well-crafted email, effective communication builds trust and fosters understanding. It's not just about selling a product, it's about conveying a vision, demonstrating value, creating a position of difference and forging a relationship that transcends the transaction.

5. Resilience and perseverance

In the world of B2B sales, rejection is not the exception but the norm. A strong work ethic helps salespeople maintain resilience in the face of setbacks, keeping a positive mindset even when opportunities fall through. Rejection should be viewed as an opportunity to learn, adjust the approach, and come back stronger. Perseverance is the fuel that propels successful salespeople forward. It's the determination to weather the storms of uncertainty, overcome objections, and persist in the pursuit of their goals. This resilience, coupled with an unwavering belief in the value they bring, distinguishes truly successful B2B salespeople.

6. Customer-centric focus

A customer-centric focus is not just a catchphrase; it's a guiding principle for successful B2B salespeople. They prioritise the needs and satisfaction of their customers. This focus extends beyond the initial sale, encompassing post-purchase support and ongoing relationship-building. Customer satisfaction is not merely a metric for successful salespeople; it is a measure of their effectiveness in understanding and meeting the evolving needs of their customers. A commitment to customer success translates into repeat business, referrals, and a reputation as a credible person.

7. Data-driven decision-making

In the age of big data, leveraging analytics to inform decisions is crucial. Successful B2B salespeople harness data to understand their environment, evaluate the effectiveness of their strategies, and identify opportunities for improvement. This analytical approach extends to the individual sales process, where data guides the allocation of resources, the identification of high-potential leads, and the measurement of key performance indicators. Data-driven decision-making is not just about numbers; it's about gaining insights that inform strategic choices. Recognising the power of data helps salespeople refine and adapt their approach and stay ahead in a competitive landscape.

8. Team collaboration

B2B sales success (or failure) is seldom a solo endeavour. Successful salespeople recognise the value of collaboration, not only within their own sales team but across departments within their organisation. They work seamlessly with marketing, product development, and customer support teams, fostering a collaborative culture that aligns everyone toward a common goal, satisfying the customer and winning the business. Team collaboration extends to external partnerships as well, especially when collaborating with other businesses to provide comprehensive solutions or forging strategic alliances. Successful B2B salespeople understand the strength that comes from great teamwork.

9. Ethical conduct

I can't stress enough that Integrity forms the bedrock of being successful in B2B sales. Trust is fragile and ethical conduct is the glue that binds lasting relationships. Successful salespeople set great store by transparency, honesty, and fairness in all their interactions, even if telling the truth loses the deal. Ethical conduct extends to how they represent their organisation, handle confidential information, and navigate complex negotiations. It's not just about closing deals; it's about building a reputation for reliability and integrity that seeps into your personal brand and extends throughout your career.

10. Asking for the order

The final thing to mention, is that successful salespeople know when and how to ask for the order, which if everything else is done correctly is not only the most rewarding point of the sales cycle, but also (should be) the easiest to do.

In conclusion, the characteristics of a successful B2B salesperson are multifaceted, combining the art of human connection with the science of strategic thinking and data-driven decision-making.

Anyone embarking on a B2B sales career must seek to refine their existing skills, remembering that these must be cultivated and honed consistently, contributing (hopefully) to a career marked by continuous growth and success.

Chapter 3: Building your personal brand

"Your brand is what people say about you when you're not in the room." – Jeff Bezos

Your personal brand is your calling card. It's not just about what you sell; it's about who you are, how you conduct yourself and the value you bring to every interaction. In an industry where trust, credibility and relationships are paramount, building a strong personal brand can be the key to standing out in a crowded marketplace.

Your personal brand is how others perceive you. It's the culmination of your skills, actions and reputation.

A strong personal brand is built over time, through consistency, authenticity, and a genuine commitment to excellence. In this chapter, I'll explore practical and thoughtful ways to build and sustain your personal brand that not only elevates your career, but also leaves a positive, lasting impression on everyone you meet.

So what are the key principles for building your personal brand?

1. Be good at what you do

Competence is the foundation of a strong personal brand. People will naturally want to associate with you if you're consistently good at what you do and deliver value to them. This means dedicating time to honing your craft, practicing and always striving to improve.

How to achieve this?

- Work hard: Success doesn't happen by accident. Dedicate time to mastering your industry, products and processes.
- Embrace lifelong learning: Stay curious and seek opportunities to grow. Attend training sessions, read industry publications and learn from your peers.
- Seek feedback: Regularly ask for feedback to identify areas for improvement and to demonstrate your commitment to growth.

Why it matters.

When you're recognised for your expertise, people will naturally trust you and your recommendations. Competence builds credibility and opens doors to new opportunities.

2. Be humble

While confidence is essential in sales, boastfulness is not. Humility is an endearing quality that helps you build rapport and meaningful connections. Nobody wants to work with a braggart who constantly talks about their achievements without acknowledging others.

How to achieve this?

- Celebrate others' successes as much as your own. The word for this is "confelicity".
- Acknowledge when you are wrong and be willing to learn from mistakes.
- Focus conversations on others, clients, colleagues and prospects, rather than yourself.

Why it matters.

A humble demeanour shows that you value others' opinions and are open to collaboration. This makes you approachable and helps build stronger relationships.

3. Be authentic

Authenticity is non-negotiable when building a personal brand. People can sense insincerity and in the long run, those who are inauthentic and unethical are always found out. Being true to yourself not only builds trust but also makes your interactions more meaningful.

How to achieve this

- Be honest in your communications, even when it's not the easiest path
- Let your personality shine. Don't try to emulate someone you're not (or as Oscar Wilde said, *"be yourself, everyone else is taken"*).
- Stand by your values, even in challenging situations.

Why it matters

When you're authentic, you create genuine connections. People trust and respect those who are real, making them more likely to buy from you and recommend you to others.

4. Be brave

Courage is a vital trait in B2B sales. There will be times when doing the right thing might come at a personal cost - perhaps it's being honest about a product's limitations or admitting when you don't have all the answers. Being brave enough to prioritise your reputation over the result is essential.

How to achieve this.

- Admit when you don't know something, but commit to finding the answers.
- Speak up for a client's best interests, even if it means challenging internal processes or colleagues.
- Take calculated risks when pursuing opportunities outside your comfort zone.

Why it matters.

Bravery fosters respect and trust. It shows you are willing to put others' needs above your own and that you prioritise long-term success over short-term gains.

5. Be kind

Kindness is a quality that is often overlooked in the competitive world of sales, but it's one of the most powerful traits you can cultivate. Treat everyone, clients, colleagues, and competitors with respect and empathy.

How to achieve this.

- Approach every interaction with patience and understanding.
- Assume positive intent, even when people make mistakes.
- Offer help without expecting anything in return.

Why it matters.

Kindness builds goodwill and strengthens relationships. People are more likely to want to work with someone who makes them feel respected and valued.

6. Be curious, not judgmental (attributed to Walt Whitman and Ted Lasso)

This was something that came late to me and I wish I'd switched onto it much earlier. If I had, I would not only have been a better salesperson, but I'd also have been a better human. Over the years I've sometimes been too quick to judge others – and sometimes others have been too quick to judge me. No one benefitted.

Curiosity is the key to understanding others, while judgment often creates unnecessary barriers. Embrace a mindset seeking to understand before forming opinions.

How to achieve this.

- Ask open-ended questions and practice active listening to learn about others' perspectives.
- Avoid jumping to conclusions. Take the time to gather context.
- Reflect on past situations where judgment clouded your thinking, and consider how curiosity could have led to better outcomes.

Why it matters.

Curiosity opens doors to new opportunities and helps you build rapport and deeper connections. It demonstrates that you are genuinely interested in understanding others' needs and challenges.

7. Ask intelligent questions and actively listen to the answers

The ability to ask intelligent questions and truly listen to the answers is a skill that sets top sales people apart. It allows them to uncover valuable insights, and find out what is of true value to the customer.

How to achieve this.

- Prepare questions that show your understanding of the customer's industry and challenges.
- Listen actively. Don't interrupt or think about your response while the other person is speaking.
- Summarise what you've heard to confirm understanding and show that you value their input.

Why it matters.

When you ask intelligent questions and listen actively, you increase your credibility by gaining a deeper understanding of your clients' needs, allowing you to provide better solutions.

8. Do what you say you're going to do

Reliability is a cornerstone of a strong personal brand. Following through on commitments, big or small, demonstrates professionalism and builds trust.

How to achieve this.

- Set realistic expectations and communicate clearly if timelines need to change.
- Keep track of commitments. If the timescales are going to slip let others know early.
- Prioritise quality over speed. Doing it right is better than rushing to meet a deadline.

Why it matters.

When people know they can count on you, they're more likely to trust you with bigger opportunities. Consistency in delivering on promises reinforces your credibility and strengthens your relationships.

Additional thoughts for success.

- Be visible. Engage on professional platforms like LinkedIn, share your insights, and connect with peers to increase your visibility.
- Embrace feedback. Use constructive feedback as a tool for growth, not as a personal critique.
- Stay consistent. Your brand is built over time through repeated actions. Ensure your behaviour aligns with your values every day.

How to use a personal development plan to assist your progress

A personal development plan is a structured approach to developing your personal brand, achieving your objective and your broader career aspirations. It's a practical tool for ensuring your personal brand evolves in the direction you want.

How to achieve this.

- Set clear goals. Identify specific areas for improvement that support your personal brand, such as communication, collaboration, leadership or specific knowledge areas.
- Break it down. Divide larger goals into manageable milestones and create an actionable roadmap to achieve them.
- Seek feedback. Regularly review your progress with mentors, colleagues and trusted friends who can provide constructive feedback.

- Update regularly. Treat your personal development plan as a living document. Revisit and refine it as you grow and your goals evolve.

Why it matters.

A personal development plan helps you stay focused and intentional in building your personal brand. It ensures that your development efforts are aligned with the image you want to project and allows you to track measurable progress over time. By committing to continuous improvement, you are demonstrating a proactive and disciplined approach to personal growth, qualities that inspire trust and respect in others.

Bringing it all together

Building your personal brand in B2B sales isn't just about crafting a polished image, it's about being the best version of yourself and consistently delivering value to those around you.

By embracing these characteristics, you'll not only differentiate yourself from competitors, but also create meaningful connections that drive long-term success.

Start today by practicing the principles outlined in this chapter and remember that every interaction is an opportunity to leave a positive, (or negative) lasting impression. Success in B2B sales isn't just about closing deals, it's about becoming the person people want to buy from, trust and recommend to others.

Chapter 4: Understanding the B2B sales cycle

"People don't buy products; they buy solutions to their problems." – Theodore Levitt

Navigating the B2B sales cycle requires a comprehensive understanding of its unique stages and complexities. Unlike consumer sales, the B2B sales process involves longer timelines, higher stakes, and multiple decision-makers. Each step demands strategic thinking, relationship-building and a deep knowledge of both the customer's needs and the value your solution brings.

What is the B2B sales cycle?

The B2B sales cycle refers to the structured process through which a business sells products or services to another business. This process typically includes distinct stages, each of which plays a crucial role in moving a prospect closer to becoming a customer. The cycle's length and complexity often depend on the industry, the size of the deal, and the organisational dynamics of the buying company.

Understanding the sales cycle is critical for optimising efforts and achieving consistent results. By identifying where a prospect is within the cycle, sales professionals can tailor their approach and improve their chances of closing the deal.

Key stages of the B2B sales cycle

1. Prospecting

The first step in the B2B sales cycle is identifying potential customers. Effective prospecting involves:

- Researching target companies and industries.
- Using tools such as CRM platforms and LinkedIn to identify prospect organisations and people.
- Qualifying leads based on predefined criteria such as industry, company size, and potential need for your solution and their fit to your ideal customer profile (more on this later).

Prospecting lays the foundation for success by ensuring sales efforts are focused on producing a continuous flow of closeable opportunities.

2. Initial contact

Once a prospect is identified, the next step is to initiate contact. This can take various forms, including cold emails, phone calls, networking at industry events or (best of all), by referral. The goal is to introduce your company, demonstrate value, and establish a relationship.

Key strategies for effective initial contact include:

- Personalising your outreach to address the prospect's specific challenges.
- Clearly articulating how your solution can solve their pain points.
- Setting a tone of collaboration and trust.

Don't lead your initial contact with what you do, lead with how you can help the prospect through the value you add.

3. Qualification

During the qualification phase, the focus shifts to understanding the prospect's unique needs, goals and challenges. This stage is crucial for building rapport and gathering information that will inform your sales strategy.

Discovery questions to consider include:

- What are the prospect's top priorities?
- What problems are they trying to solve?
- What outcomes do they expect from a potential solution?

By deeply understanding their situation and asking the right questions, you position yourself as a trusted advisor rather than merely someone who wants to sell them something.

4. Solution design

The solution design stage bridges the gap between understanding your prospect's needs and presenting a tailored solution. This phase is where you bring together everything learned during qualification - customer personality, challenges, goals and priorities - to craft a solution that speaks directly to their needs. It's also your opportunity to differentiate yourself from the competition.

Things to consider during solution design include:

- How does the customer's personality influence their decision-making? Are they data-driven, relationship-focused, risk-averse?
- What specific problem are they seeking to solve by investing in your solution?
- How can you align your solution with their desired outcomes and business goals?
- What unique features or approaches can you highlight to stand out from competitors?

By tailoring your solution to reflect what you've discovered about the customer, you show that you've listened and understand their unique situation. Use this stage to emphasise how your offering is not only a fit for their needs, but also a superior choice compared to alternatives.

A well-designed solution demonstrates that you're more than a salesperson, you're a problem solver who genuinely cares about the customer's success. By integrating their personality, challenges, and priorities into your proposal, you build trust and increase the likelihood of winning the deal. Moreover, thoughtful differentiation can make your solution the obvious choice in a crowded marketplace.

5. Proposal and presentation

With a clear understanding of the prospect's needs, the next step is to present your solution. This stage often involves a formal proposal, presentation and product demonstration.

Best practices include:

- Tailoring your proposal and presentation to align with the prospect's pain points and goals.
- Highlighting key benefits and differentiators of your solution.
- Using storytelling and case studies to illustrate the value you bring.

A compelling proposal and presentation demonstrates not only the technical capabilities of your solution but also its strategic value to the customer.

6. Handling objections

No B2B sales cycle is complete without addressing objections. Common objections might relate to price, timing, or perceived fit. This stage requires active listening, empathy, and a problem-solving mindset. Objections should be seen as buying signals because people only ever ask questions about things they are genuinely interested in.

Tips for overcoming objections include:

- Validate the prospect's concerns and provide clear, data-driven responses.
- Offer alternative solutions or concessions where appropriate.
- Reaffirm the unique value your solution brings to their organisation.

Addressing objections effectively builds confidence and keeps the deal moving forward.

7. Negotiation

In the negotiation phase, the focus shifts to aligning on terms that work for both parties (win-win). This might involve discussions around pricing, implementation timelines, or service-level agreements.

Key elements of successful negotiation include:

- Being prepared with a clear understanding of your solution's value and limits.
- Seeking a win-win outcome that aligns with the prospect's priorities.
- Maintaining transparency and professionalism throughout the process.
- Protecting your profit margin.

Negotiation is often where trust and rapport built earlier in the cycle pays dividends.

8. Closing the deal

The closing stage is where verbal agreements are formalised and contracts are signed. Successful closings often hinge on clear communication and thorough preparation.

Steps to facilitate a smooth closing include:

- Reiterate the agreed value and terms.
- Ensure all stakeholders are aligned and have the necessary approvals.
- Address any last-minute concerns promptly.

Closing marks the culmination of the sales cycle, but it's also the beginning of the customer relationship.

9. Post-sale follow-up and support

A successful B2B sales cycle doesn't end with the contract. The post-sale phase is critical for ensuring customer satisfaction and setting the stage for future opportunities.

Key actions include:

- Providing onboarding support to ensure smooth implementation.
- Following up regularly to address any issues and measure satisfaction.
- Identifying future cross-sell, upsell and referral opportunities.

A proactive approach to post-sale engagement strengthens relationships and drives long-term value.

Common challenges in the B2B sales cycle:

1. Managing lengthy sales cycles

B2B sales often take months or even years to complete. To maintain momentum,

- Set clear milestones and regularly review progress
- Keep communication consistent and value driven
- Use CRM tools and sales pipeline management tools to stay organised and track interactions.

2. Navigating multiple decision-makers

B2B purchases typically involve input from various stakeholders, each with different priorities. To manage this complexity,

- Map out the decision-making hierarchy and the buying roles of each.
- Tailor your messaging to address the concerns of each stakeholder.
- Identify and cultivate internal champions who can advocate for your solution.

3. Differentiating in competitive markets

Standing out in a crowded market is a perennial challenge. To differentiate effectively,

- Highlight your unique value propositions and success stories.
- Leverage industry insights and thought leadership.
- Build strong, personalised relationships with prospects.

Understanding the B2B sales cycle is essential for navigating its challenges and capitalising on its opportunities. By mastering each stage, from prospecting to post-sale follow-up, salespeople can build trust, deliver value and drive meaningful results. A structured, customer-focused approach not only improves win rates but also fosters lasting partnerships.

The B2B Sale Cycle

A key point to remember is that opportunities in the B2B sales cycle are ever present. Most (if not all organisations) are always planning investments that will help them do one or more of three things,

- To become more profitable
- To improve operational effectiveness
- To enhance or protect their brand and reputation.

Consistent and disciplined prospecting within your ideal customer target market and your existing accounts increases your chances of influencing the outcome by engaging early in the process.

Be proactive.

Chapter 5: The decision-making process

"In complex sales, it's not about selling to one person but enabling consensus across the entire decision-making group." – Brent Adamson.

In the world of complex B2B sales, success hinges not on persuading a single individual but on enabling consensus across an often-diverse group known as the decision-making group (or unit). Fully understanding the nuances and subtleties of this process is critical to aligning your sales strategy and activity with your prospect's decision-making journey.

Decision-making vs. basis of decision vs. approval

Before we explore further, it's important to distinguish between three parts of the sales process journey that are often confused with each other; the decision-making process, the basis of the decision and the approval to proceed. Whilst inextricably interconnected, these are distinct steps the prospect will engage in (we will take a closer look at the "basis of decision" in the next chapter); the key differences are:

1. The decision-making process

- Description: Refers to the steps taken by your prospect to evaluate and select a preferred solution. This includes identifying needs, evaluating options and reaching consensus among the people in the decision-making unit.
- Who's involved: Decision-makers, recommenders, users and gatekeepers
- Example: A cross-departmental team evaluates potential outsourced call centre solutions based on functionality, scalability, integration with existing systems and cultural fit. After which they nominate a preferred supplier.

2. Basis of decision

- Description: Refers to the criteria and drivers for influencing the final choice, such as, return on investment (ROI), compatibility, vendor trust, risk mitigation and personal drivers. In other words, does your solution satisfy the objectives of the organisation and the personal preferences of the individuals in the decision-making unit.
- Who's involved: Primarily recommenders and decision-makers, often with input from users.
- Example: The organisation's decision-making unit selects a vendor offering the best ROI, competitive price and backed by strong customer references. The key influencers

in the decision-making unit team feel there is a better cultural fit with them from you compared to your competitions; hence even though the material offers have little between them, you win by being personally preferred.

3. Approval

- Description: Refers to the procedural step where the chosen solution is formally sanctioned. This involves budgetary authorisations and compliance checks.
- Who's Involved: Finance teams, procurement, legal departments and senior executives; the higher the relative investment to the size of organisation you are dealing with, the higher up the organisation the approvers will be
- Example: Once the decision is made, the procurement team ensures the solution complies with legal and financial requirements before final approval.

Understanding the decision-making process

The decision-making process in complex B2B sales is rarely linear. Each organisation's approach differs based on their internal structures, short-term objectives, long-term goals, and priorities. Knowing this process is essential because your sales activities must align with the buyer's timeline. For instance, there's no point submitting a proposal tomorrow if the decision is six months away and the organisation is still in the discovery phase. Your strategy should mirror their progress, ensuring you're present and relevant at every key milestone.

Five key decision-making process questions

1. **Timeline.**
   Have you matched your sales campaign activity plan to the prospect's decision-making process timeline, thus avoiding wasted efforts and premature actions?
2. **Key milestones.**
   Have you identified critical stages such as discovery, evaluation and decision to plan your engagement effectively?

3. **Prospect journey awareness.**
   Are you aware of internal shifts or delays within the prospect's business that will require you to adjust your sales plan timelines (and your forecast)?

4. **Real-time input.**

- The approval came from the sales director after the procurement team signed off on cost and compliance.

Key insights

The size and structure of the organisation significantly influenced the sales process. In small companies, decisions are faster and more direct, often hinging on personal relationships and immediate needs. In large companies, patience and strategic engagement with a diverse decision-making unit are crucial to navigating complex layers and aligning with formal approval processes.

Understanding the size and structure of the organisation helps you adapt your approach to align with their specific decision-making dynamics.

Who makes the final decision?

One of the biggest risks in complex sales is assuming the person you're speaking with has full decision-making authority when they don't.

To avoid this pitfall, never directly ask, "who is the decision-maker?" If they say, "it's me" and they're not it's a difficult spot to escape from. For example, you can hardly respond with "I don't believe you". Instead, use a more subtle approach.

When I'm seeking to qualify a decision-making process, this is the question I ask. *"I deal with lots of organisations, large and small across a broad range of industries. Each has its own unique decision-making process for projects like these. How does it work in your company?"* The benefit of framing the question like this is,

- It encourages the prospect to share valuable details about their organisation's process.
- It helps you identify all key stakeholders and their roles.
- It positions you as someone genuinely interested in understanding the company's internal workings rather than making assumptions or taking things for granted
- It demonstrates your experience and credibility by acknowledging the diversity of decision-making approaches across industries.

In most companies, more often than not there is only one true decision-maker, even in a complex consensus-driven process. This is the person who can say "no" when everyone else in the decision-making unit team feel there is a better cultural fit with them from you compared to your competitions; hence even though the material offers have little between them, you win by being personally preferred.

3. Approval

- Description: Refers to the procedural step where the chosen solution is formally sanctioned. This involves budgetary authorisations and compliance checks.
- Who's Involved: Finance teams, procurement, legal departments and senior executives; the higher the relative investment to the size of organisation you are dealing with, the higher up the organisation the approvers will be
- Example: Once the decision is made, the procurement team ensures the solution complies with legal and financial requirements before final approval.

Understanding the decision-making process

The decision-making process in complex B2B sales is rarely linear. Each organisation's approach differs based on their internal structures, short-term objectives, long-term goals, and priorities. Knowing this process is essential because your sales activities must align with the buyer's timeline. For instance, there's no point submitting a proposal tomorrow if the decision is six months away and the organisation is still in the discovery phase. Your strategy should mirror their progress, ensuring you're present and relevant at every key milestone.

Five key decision-making process questions

1. **Timeline.**
   Have you matched your sales campaign activity plan to the prospect's decision-making process timeline, thus avoiding wasted efforts and premature actions?
2. **Key milestones.**
   Have you identified critical stages such as discovery, evaluation and decision to plan your engagement effectively?

3. **Prospect journey awareness.**
   Are you aware of internal shifts or delays within the prospect's business that will require you to adjust your sales plan timelines (and your forecast)?

4. **Real-time input.**

Have you mapped out how each stage of the prospect's decision-making process may involve different levels of input from various members of the decision-making unit, depending on their expertise and experience?

5. **Decision criteria validation.**
   Have you confirmed the key factors driving the prospect's decision-making process, such as ROI, compliance, scalability, cultural alignment or anything else? Are these criteria influencing how the decision-making unit prioritises options? What would your answer be to the question "why should we buy from you?"

Decision-making and approval in small vs. large companies

At this stage, it's also worth expanding on the point that the decision-making and approval process varies significantly between small and large organisations. Moreover, the larger the organisation and their planned investment, the more complex the decision-making unit will be and the higher up the organisational hierarchy the approval will be. A general view that can be adopted is as follows.

Small companies

- Decision-making processes are typically faster due to fewer stakeholders and may be limited to a single person
- The decision-maker may also play multiple roles (decision-maker and user)
- Processes are often less formal, with more direct communication.

Large companies

- Involves multiple stakeholders across departments with varying organisational and personal priorities.
- Decisions can take longer due to hierarchical layers and formal procedures.
- Compliance processes, such as procurement and legal, may (and often do) play a larger role.

A tale of two sales

Let me illustrate this with two contrasting examples from my own personal experience. I once sold a £40,000 sales training package to two different companies: a small business with a £10m turnover and 40 employees, and a larger organisation with a £200m turnover and 400 employees. The same package, but two very different journeys.

The small company

The decision-maker in the small business was the managing director, who also doubled as the recommender of the preferred solution to the company's sales director. After our initial meeting, it was clear that they needed immediate solutions to boost their team's performance. The sales director wanted to place the order with an organisation he had used before. However, the MD preferred the johnpc ltd solution and approved the deal within a week. The process was direct and informal, a conversation, a proposal, and a handshake.

Key characteristics

- The MD played multiple roles: decision-maker, recommender (and user - they attended all the workshops)
- No formal procurement process was required
- The decision was driven by an urgent need and trust in my expertise and reputation.

The larger company

In the larger organisation, the journey was far more complex. The decision-making unit included HR, sales leadership, and procurement. Each stakeholder had different priorities. HR focused on team development, sales on capability improvement and procurement on cost compliance. The process took six months, involving multiple meetings, presentations, and rounds of negotiation before I finally closed the deal.

Key characteristics

- The decision-making unit comprised distinct roles: decision-maker (sales director), recommenders (HR and sales managers) and gatekeepers (procurement).
- A formal RFP (request for proposal) process was required and compliance with this was mandatory.

- The approval came from the sales director after the procurement team signed off on cost and compliance.

Key insights

The size and structure of the organisation significantly influenced the sales process. In small companies, decisions are faster and more direct, often hinging on personal relationships and immediate needs. In large companies, patience and strategic engagement with a diverse decision-making unit are crucial to navigating complex layers and aligning with formal approval processes.

Understanding the size and structure of the organisation helps you adapt your approach to align with their specific decision-making dynamics.

Who makes the final decision?

One of the biggest risks in complex sales is assuming the person you're speaking with has full decision-making authority when they don't.

To avoid this pitfall, never directly ask, "who is the decision-maker?" If they say, "it's me" and they're not it's a difficult spot to escape from. For example, you can hardly respond with "I don't believe you". Instead, use a more subtle approach.

When I'm seeking to qualify a decision-making process, this is the question I ask. *"I deal with lots of organisations, large and small across a broad range of industries. Each has its own unique decision-making process for projects like these. How does it work in your company?"* The benefit of framing the question like this is,

- It encourages the prospect to share valuable details about their organisation's process.
- It helps you identify all key stakeholders and their roles.
- It positions you as someone genuinely interested in understanding the company's internal workings rather than making assumptions or taking things for granted
- It demonstrates your experience and credibility by acknowledging the diversity of decision-making approaches across industries.

In most companies, more often than not there is only one true decision-maker, even in a complex consensus-driven process. This is the person who can say "no" when everyone else says "yes", and can say "yes" when everyone else says no. Identifying this individual early can streamline your efforts and ensure your solution aligns with their priorities.

In many B2B complex sales scenarios, the decision-making unit comprises multiple stakeholders, including recommenders, users, and gatekeepers. However, the ultimate decision of who wins or loses typically rests with a single individual, the decision-maker. While approvals might require committees to verify compliance, budgets or legalities, the final call on selecting a preferred supplier is made by this individual.

it is essential to recognise that not all stakeholders in the decision-making unit have equal influence or authority. While several roles may contribute to the evaluation process, their input serves different purposes. Understanding these distinctions enables you to address the right concerns and focus your efforts effectively. Usually, the decision-making unit comprises three broad roles:

- Decision-maker: The individual who decides which supplier is the best fit. This person is often a senior executive who evaluates the strategic alignment and long-term implications of the choice
- Recommenders and influencers (users): Help shape the decision-maker's view but ultimately do not have the authority to make the final call
- Gatekeepers: Ensure compliance to procedures and allocated budgets.

A personal experience

I remember selling a £250,000 communications network to a large organisation. The decision-making unit was extensive, including IT managers, procurement officers, and department heads, each with distinct priorities. The IT team scrutinised technical compatibility, procurement focused on cost and department heads voiced operational needs. While each group had a say, I quickly identified that the chief information officer (CIO) held the final authority to make the decision.

I tailored my messaging to align with her strategic goals (scalability and reliability) through regular engagement and I secured her buy-in. Despite the procurement team's initial pushback on price, the CIO's decision overrode objections. The deal was approved after compliance and budgetary checks, but the choice to move forward was solely hers.

A practical example

Imagine a scenario where a company is purchasing a new CRM system. The decision-making unit includes the IT manager, sales director and procurement officer.

- The IT manager evaluates technical compatibility and operational feasibility.
- The sales director focuses on ease of use, functionality and how the CRM will support revenue growth.
- The procurement officer ensures the solution is cost-effective and compliant with purchasing policies.

In the end, the sales director as the ultimate decision-maker chooses the CRM vendor based on strategic priorities, ease of use for the sales team and reporting functionality. Following which in the approval process the CEO then sanctions the contract, despite being neither the decision-maker nor involved in the decision-making process.

Recognising the true decision-maker early allows you to tailor your messaging and build a relationship with the individual whose priorities will ultimately shape the outcome. Engage with the entire decision-making unit, but always ensure you are addressing the short-term objectives, long-term goals, concerns, and vision of the one person who holds the final say.

Identifying and engaging with the decision-making unit members

In high-value sales, the decision-making unit is a dynamic group of stakeholders, each with a unique role in influencing the outcome. Understanding these roles is critical to navigating complex sales cycles effectively. By identifying and addressing the priorities of each stakeholder, you can craft tailored approaches that resonate with decision-makers, recommenders, users and gatekeepers alike, ensuring no critical perspective is overlooked.

The key characteristics to help you identify the roles people play and how to engage with them is as follows,

1. Decision-maker characteristics

- The individual with the final authority to approve or reject the deal.
- Can override the group consensus, saying no when everyone else says yes and yes when everyone else says no.
- Typically occupies a senior position, especially for higher value deals
- Vision tends to be long-term and strategic.

How to engage

- Focus on aligning your solution with their strategic goals.
- Present a compelling value proposition tied to long-term benefits.
- Respect their time and deliver high-impact communication.

2. Recommender characteristics

- Trusted advisors to the decision-maker with strong credibility.
- Can include one or more individuals.
- They can influence decisions but lack final authority
- Vision is short to medium-term and operational.

How to engage

- Build trust through transparency and reliability.
- Equip them with materials to advocate for your solution internally.
- Address their operational concerns to strengthen their case.

3. User characteristics

- Direct users or those impacted by the product or service.
- Often represented by multiple people.
- Key to driving adoption and repeat business post-sale.
- Vision is short-term and operational.

How to engage

- Highlight user-centric benefits such as ease of use and efficiency.
- Involve them in demonstrations or pilot programs.
- Show how your solution solves their immediate challenges.

4. Gatekeeper characteristics

- Often from departments like procurement, finance, or legal.
- Enforces compliance with organisational processes.
- Can delay or block access to the decision-maker.
- Lacks authority to decide but controls access.

How to engage

- Respect their processes and provide necessary documentation promptly.
- Build rapport to reduce friction in approvals.
- Demonstrate compliance with organisational policies.

The decision-making unit activity

The activity the decision-making unit members engage in is dictated by their organisation purchasing cycle. As such, the following is offered as a general guideline.

The customer's purchasing cycle is driven by their need to address a strategic or operational challenge. Success in pursuing sales opportunities relies on aligning your sales process with the customer's activity focus and decision-making journey. Understanding this allows you to build a competitive advantage, accelerate decision-making and bypass unnecessary delays.

Key factors influencing success include the strength of relationships, alignment with the target market profile, solution fit to the customer's needs, the skill of the salesperson, the tools at their disposal, and the robustness of their sales methodology. It's not one factor but the interplay of all these elements that determines success.

Stages of the customer's decision-making cycle

1. Active and informal supplier dialogue

- Prospect focus: The customer identifies a requirement for change, whether strategic or operational
- Your role: Build rapport and establish yourself as a trusted advisor during early, informal discussions.

2. Needs definition

- Prospect focus: The customer explores solution options, both in-house and external, to define their needs.
- Your role: Help articulate their requirements and demonstrate how your solution can address their objectives.

3. Internal justification

- Prospect focus: The customer prepares a business case, seeks financial approval and evaluates ROI.
- Your role: Provide supporting data, case studies and ROI analysis to strengthen their internal justification.

4. Solutions evaluation

- Prospect focus: The decision-making unit actively reviews options, evaluates solutions, and defines the basis of decision criteria.
- Your role: Engage with all stakeholders in the decision-making unit, address their concerns, and highlight how your solution meets their criteria.

5. Formal prospective supplier dialogue

- Prospect focus: The purchasing process becomes formal, with detailed specifications and engagement with potential suppliers.
- Your role: Submit a tailored proposal, address questions and participate actively in the formal process.

6. Preferred suppliers

- Prospect focus: The customer shortlists suppliers that meet the basis of decision criteria.
- Your role: Continue differentiating your offering, reinforcing trust, and addressing any lingering objections.

7. Chosen supplier nominated

- Prospects focus: The decision-making process concludes with the nomination of the chosen supplier. Final proposals, detailed negotiations, and Best and Final Offers (BAFO) occur at this stage.
- Your role: Excel in negotiations, present a compelling BAFO, and secure the close.

8. Contract award and project delivery

- Prospect focus: The contract is awarded, and project delivery begins. Post-contract adjustments and changes may occur.

- Your role: Ensure smooth implementation, maintain communication, and deliver on promises to set the stage for long-term success.

Understanding the decision-making process in high-value complex B2B sales is a prime example of sales as an art and a science.

By identifying the roles within the decision-making unit, aligning your timeline with the prospects decision-making journey and distinguishing between decision-making and approval, you position yourself as a trusted advisor capable of navigating the complexities of the process.

Remember, your success lies in enabling consensus while addressing the unique needs and priorities of every stakeholder involved.

Exercise: Understanding the decision-making process

Objective: To analyse and navigate a prospect's decision-making process effectively by identifying key stages, stakeholders, and their roles.

Step 1: Select a target prospect

- Identify a current or hypothetical prospect relevant to your sales efforts.

Step 2: Map the prospect's decision-making process

Using the **stages of the customer's decision-making cycle** as a reference, answer the following questions:

- What stage of the decision-making process is the prospect currently in? (needs definition, solutions evaluation, preferred supplier nomination)?
- What is the estimated timeline for their process and how can you align your actions with it?

Step 3: Identify the decision-making unit

For the chosen prospect, list out potential stakeholders and their roles in the process. Use these categories as a guide:

- Decision-maker: Who has the final say?

- Recommenders/influencers: Who will shape the decision but lacks final authority?
- Users: Who will directly interact with your solution?
- Gatekeepers: Who controls access, compliance, or budgetary processes?

Step 4: Develop stakeholder-specific actions

For each stakeholder, identify one actionable step you can take to engage with them effectively. For example,

- Decision-maker: Craft a value proposition highlighting long-term strategic benefits.
- Recommenders: Provide tailored materials (case studies) to support their advocacy.
- Users: Arrange a product demonstration or pilot to address usability concerns.
- Gatekeepers: Ensure compliance by delivering all required documentation promptly.

Step 5: Analyse key milestones

Using the information gathered, determine the following:

- What are the critical milestones in the decision-making process (e.g., evaluation completion, shortlist creation)?
- How can you proactively address potential bottlenecks or delays at these milestones?

Practice makes perfect

Reflect on your findings and strategies using the following prompts:

- Alignment: Does your sales activity plan align with the prospect's decision-making timeline and process?
- Stakeholder engagement: Are there gaps in your approach to addressing the needs and concerns of all members of the decision-making unit?
- Next steps: Based on this exercise, what is one actionable change you can make to strengthen your position in the sales process?

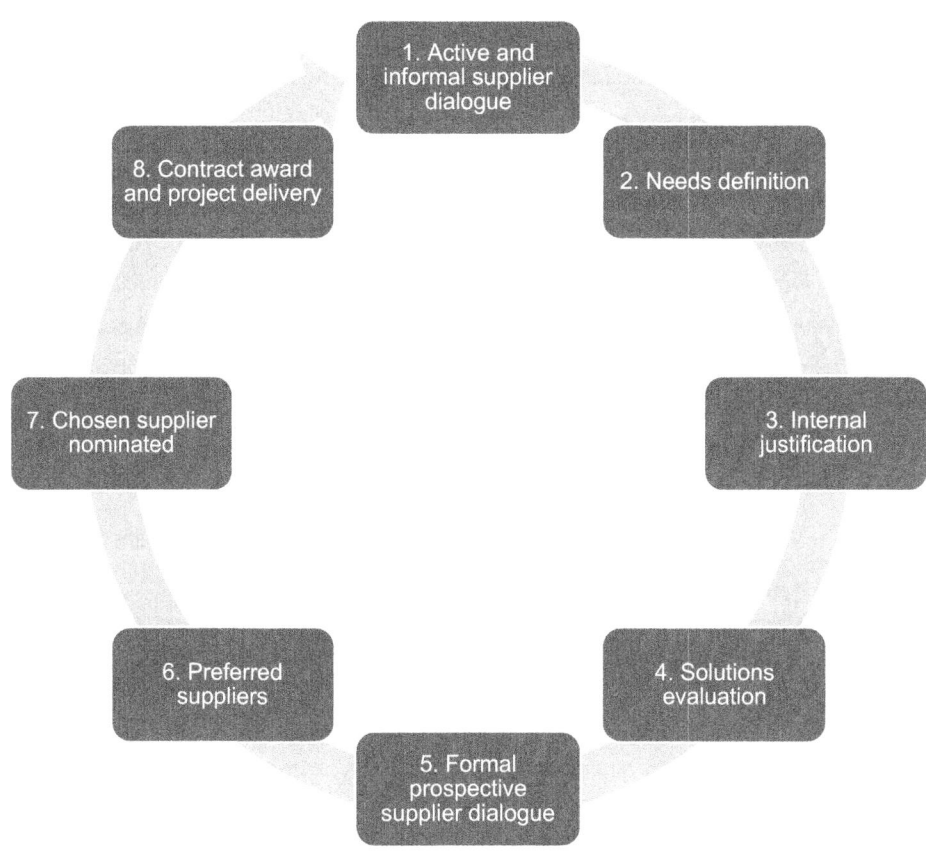

The B2B prospects decision-making journey

Chapter 6: The basis of decision

"Decisions are made based on logic and validated with emotion." – Simon Sinek.

In the world of B2B sales, the basis on which decisions are made are complex. The higher the value of the deal and the more strategically important it is to the customer's business, the more complex decision-making can become.

Unlike individual consumer purchases, which often stem from personal desires and needs, B2B sales are driven by organisational objectives, broader accountability and carry a need for justification.

To understand the basis of decision in B2B sales, it's essential to explore the core drivers, align them with psychological frameworks such as Maslow's hierarchy of needs and examine the stark distinctions from personal purchasing behaviours. This will enable you to focus on what's most important to your prospect and their organisation.

The nature of personal purchasing decisions

When individuals make purchasing decisions, they are typically guided by their own needs or wants. These can be categorised broadly into two types of needs and wants.

Essential needs: Food, water, shelter, clothing and other basic necessities that align with the foundational levels of Maslow's hierarchy of needs. These purchases are often non-negotiable and are driven by survival and basic functionality.

Discretionary wants: Items like luxury cars, holidays or high-end technology. These purchases often serve as a means of self-actualisation or esteem-building. A person's decision to buy a premium car might stem from a desire to reflect their success or satisfy their aesthetic preferences. The justification here could be as simple as the tagline from L'Oréal; "because you're worth it."

Personal purchasing decisions, while sometimes impulsive, are almost always autonomous. The individual and often only the individual, justifies the expense, bearing the financial consequence directly.

Core drivers of B2B purchasing decisions

In contrast, B2B purchasing decisions are influenced by broader organisational objectives and carry the requirement for collective justification. Businesses do not operate in isolation and every expenditure is scrutinized to ensure alignment with the business's needs. The primary drivers behind these decisions can be summarized into three key categories.

1. Gaining a competitive advantage (making money): Businesses invest in products or services that enable them to out-perform competitors. This could include adopting cutting-edge technology, enhancing customer experience or expanding into new markets. For example, a business might purchase advanced analytics software to gain insights that competitors lack, thereby increasing market share or profitability.

2. Operational effectiveness and efficiency (saving money): Cost reduction is a significant motivator in B2B decisions. Companies often seek solutions that streamline operations, reduce waste or improve productivity without increasing operating cost. For instance, investing in automation tools can lower labour costs while maintaining high output levels.

3. Protecting or enhancing reputation (brand management): Businesses are acutely aware of the importance of their brand's image. Decisions in this category may involve choosing eco-friendly suppliers to align with sustainability objectives or investing in cybersecurity solutions to safeguard customer data. These decisions aim to protect or enhance their organisation's reputation in the market.

The need for justification in B2B Sales

One of the defining aspects of B2B purchasing is the requirement for justification. Unlike personal luxury purchases that may rely on emotional reasoning, B2B decisions demand logical, evidence-based validation. This is primarily because of the following factors.

1. Shared accountability: In a business context, approval to spend is rarely made by a single individual. Purchasing decisions often involve multiple stakeholders, including procurement teams, finance departments and executive leadership. Each stakeholder has unique priorities and the decision must satisfy all these diverse interests. Rocking up and responding with, "*because I'm worth it*" to a question of "*why you want to spend £1m of your company's money*"? probably won't get you very far.

2. **Budgetary constraints:** Businesses operate within defined budgets. Any purchase must demonstrate a clear return on investment or risk being deprioritised. For example, a company considering a resource planning system will need to present a detailed cost-benefit enterprise analysis to justify the upfront expenditure.

3. Risk aversion: Businesses are inherently risk-averse, particularly in high-stakes industries. Any decision that could lead to financial loss, reputational harm, or operational disruption undergoes thorough evaluation. Salespeople in B2B sales must address these concerns head-on by providing robust assurances, proof of capability and support.

Decisions are not made on price

A common fallacy in B2B sales is the assumption that all decisions are made solely based on price. Over the years I've heard salespeople say, "I lost it on price", though I don't think I've ever heard anyone say, "I won it on price".

While the cost of a solution is undoubtedly a critical consideration, it is rarely the sole or even primary factor driving the decision. Instead, what matters most is the value perceived by the buyer. Value encompasses how well your solution aligns with the buyer's specific needs and challenges.

A higher-priced solution that offers greater efficiency, enhanced reputation and a competitive edge can often outweigh a lower-priced alternative that lacks these benefits. For example, a company might choose a premium software package with superior support and scalability over a cheaper option with limited features, as the long-term value justifies the higher investment.

B2B buyers are motivated by the return on investment, not just the ticket price. They weigh factors like quality, reliability, supplier reputation, and alignment with their strategic plans. The decision to invest in a solution is ultimately about achieving outcomes that create tangible and intangible benefits, making price a single piece in a much larger puzzle.

Doubts, fears and concerns

When organisations are making high-value investments, the personal reputations of those responsible for making the decision and approving the expenditure are exposed. If they get it right and the project is a success they may receive a "well done", but if it goes wrong they can suffer personal damage to their reputation.

It's worth bearing in mind the psychological pressures that the individuals in the decision-making unit will be under and the questions they will ask themselves. These include:

Functional

- Is this product a good fit for me/my organisation?
- How reliable is the service?
- How can I be sure it really works?

Financial

- Will it make or save money for my organisation?
- Are there better priced options?
- Can I justify the return on investment to others?

Psychological

- Will buying it make me look competent or incompetent?
- What will others / my boss think?
- What happens if the plan goes wrong?

Social

- Who else is using it?
- Do organisations like mine use it?
- Will it damage or enhance my organisation's reputation?

It's unlikely that your prospect will share these with you as clearly as they are laid out above, but by asking the right questions throughout the qualification of the opportunity you can unearth what factors are of most concern and address them.

Asking questions

Asking the right questions is critical to qualifying an organization's needs and understanding the individual priorities within the decision-making unit. Thoughtful questions help uncover the basis of decision, establish trust and qualify an individual's resonating focus, a single sentence that articulates what is most important to them.

Other examples of questions to ask include:

Organisational questions:

- What are the organisation's top strategic priorities this year?
- What challenges are you currently facing in achieving these goals?
- How does your team measure success for a project like this?
- Are there any key deadlines or timelines we should be aware of?
- How does this project align with your broader business objectives (cost reduction, market expansion)?
- Are there existing systems or processes this solution needs to integrate with?

Individual stakeholder questions:

- What would a successful outcome to this project look like to you? (This is a question I use in every sales conversation and I have never had a prospect not provide an answer.
- What is your primary concern about moving forward with this project?
- How does this decision impact your role or department?
- Who else in your organisation has an interest in the outcome (and why)?

By asking these questions you achieve three things; you gain an invaluable insight into what the basis of decision will be for that individual, you make them feel that what they think is important to you and you also establish a key focus point for your sales proposal.

Linking B2B decision drivers to Maslow's hierarchy of needs

Maslow's hierarchy, though originally applied to individual motivations, offers a useful lens to understand organisational behaviour. While businesses don't have physiological needs, they do prioritise survival and growth in competitive markets. The parallels include:

- **Security needs:** Decisions aimed at risk mitigation, such as investing in insurance, cybersecurity or compliance tools align with the need for organisational safety and security.
- **Belonging and esteem needs:** Businesses strive for market recognition and partnerships, much like individuals seek social connections and esteem. Investing in public relations campaigns or certifications (like ISO standards) reflects this priority.

- **Self-actualisation:** This corresponds to innovation and thought leadership. Companies at this level prioritise visionary projects, such as adopting artificial intelligence or entering entirely new industries to realise their full potential.

Practical implications for B2B sales strategies

Understanding the basis of decision-making in B2B sales enables you to tailor your approach effectively. Here are some practical takeaways for you to consider,

- **Align sales proposals with business objectives.** Sales proposals must address one or more of the three core drivers - making money, saving money or protecting brand value. For example, instead of presenting generic features of a product, focus on how it improves efficiency by a measurable percentage or reduces costs over a specific timeframe. Offer proof statements of results achieved with other customers.
- **Build a strong business case:** Anticipate the need for justification and provide comprehensive resources to support the decision. This could include case studies, testimonials, ROI calculators, and competitive benchmarking.
- **Engage multiple stakeholders:** Identify all decision-makers involved and address their specific concerns. For instance, while a CFO might prioritise cost savings, an IT manager might focus on ease of integration and reliability.
- **Mitigate perceived risks**: Address potential objections proactively. Spend time handling known and unearthing unknown objections. Focus on alleviating concerns about product performance or implementation challenges early in the process.
- **Highlight long-term value.** Emphasise how the purchase aligns with the customer's strategic vision. For example, show how a new technology will not only reduce costs today but also position the company as an industry leader in the future. Customers are interested in achieving short-terms objectives and long-term goals. Think beyond the sale to how you can support their long-term endeavours.

The emotional underpinning of rational decisions

While B2B decisions are predominantly rational, they are not devoid of emotional underpinnings and influence. Decision-makers are human and their choices are influenced by factors like trust, confidence, personal aspirations and prior experiences and relationships. A decision-maker who feels confident in a supplier's reliability or aligns with their values is more likely to advocate for their solution within the organisation.

When I was a director at Pace communications in the 1990s, we had a requirement to buy a new fork-lift truck. Having previously worked as a salesperson for Crown Lift Trucks early in my career (and enjoyed my time there immensely), I lobbied for the order to be given to Crown, based purely on my prior relationship with the organisation. Crown won the order.

Never forget to ask the prospect if they have a preferred solution. You might learn a lot about the opportunity and about them.

Understanding the core drivers is key to a successful outcome

The basis of decision-making in B2B sales is deeply rooted in organisational priorities and collective justification. Unlike personal purchases, which can be impulsive and self-indulgent, B2B decisions are operationally or strategically focused, collaborative, and accountability driven.

By understanding the core drivers' of making money (competitive advantage), saving money (operational efficiency), protecting or enhancing reputation (brand management) and addressing the need for justification, salespeople can navigate these complex processes effectively.

Ultimately, successful B2B sales outcomes hinge on aligning your solution with the customer's challenges, building trust, demonstrating long-term value and understanding their personal motivations.

Exercise: Unearthing the basis of decision

Objective: To identify the key organisational and personal drivers influencing a decision-maker's choices.

Step 1: Choose a prospect or client

- Select a current or hypothetical B2B client.

Step 2: Ask targeted questions

Organisational Level

- What are the organisation's primary goals or challenges driving this decision? (This will help uncover whether their focus is on making money, saving money, or protecting/enhancing reputation.)

Personal level

- What does a successful outcome look like for you personally in this project?" (This question reveals the personal stakes for the decision-maker, such as reputation, job performance, or alignment with their values.)

Step 3: Identify the core drivers

Based on their responses, categorise the drivers as:

- Organisational: Competitive advantage, efficiency, or brand value.
- Personal: Functional, financial, psychological, or social concerns.

Step 4: Refine

Write down:

- How your solution addresses the organisational priorities.
- How it alleviates the personal concerns of the decision-maker.

Step 5: Reflection

Take a moment to consider:

- **Alignment:** Did the organisational and personal drivers align or were there conflicting priorities? How will you address this in your approach?
- **Key insights:** What new information did you uncover about the organisation and the decision-maker's motivations?
- **Next steps:** Based on this understanding, how will you adapt your messaging, value proposition, or proposal?

Example:

- Organisational basis of decision: Reducing operational costs by 20% this year.
- Personal basis of decision: Looking competent in front of the executive team by delivering a cost-effective solution.

Practice

Practice tailoring your value proposition to align with both organisational and personal drivers in two sentences. For example: "Our solution can reduce operational costs by 25% (organisational driver) while ensuring a smooth implementation process that will reflect positively on your leadership (personal driver)." This should be the spearpoint of your proposal and any solution presentations you deliver.

Practice makes perfect

Repeat this exercise for a different prospect and compare the outcomes. This will help you build a deeper understanding of how different organisations and individuals prioritise decisions.

Chapter 7: Identifying your ideal customer target market profile

"If you aim at everyone, you will hit no one." – Seth Godin

Understanding your ideal customer target market profile, also known as your "sweet spot," is one of the most important steps in B2B sales. Simply put, this is the specific type of customer organisation that is best suited for your products or services. When you focus on selling to the right kind of businesses, you maximise your chances of success and avoid wasting time and energy on poorly matched prospects.

To achieve this, define a list of five or six key characteristics that identify your ideal B2B customer. This gives you a clear picture of the organisations you should target and helps ensure your efforts are concentrated where they will deliver the most value. Getting this right improves your sales efficiency and effectiveness, increases your win rates and drives stronger relationships with customers who truly need what you offer.

Why this matters

Spreading your sales efforts too thin by targeting any and every organisation can lead to wasted time, frustration and underwhelming results. Without a clear focus, you risk chasing deals with companies that aren't a good fit for your offering, perhaps because of size, budget, culture, or lack of alignment with their needs.

On the other hand, when you concentrate on your "sweet spot" you can…

1. Focus your energy: Spend your time pursuing businesses that are most likely to buy.

2. Improve win rates: Sell to customers that align naturally with your value proposition.

3. Build stronger relationships: Engage with customers who genuinely benefit from your products and services.

4. Increase lifetime value: Work with organisations that are more likely to stay loyal and grow with you over time.

5. Use your internal resources effectively: Selling to your ideal customer profile means fewer wasted efforts chasing mismatched prospects.

Defining a clear target market profile isn't about limiting your opportunities; it's about working smarter and maximising your success.

Identifying the five or six key characteristics

To define your ideal B2B customer, start by outlining the specific characteristics that consistently appear in the organisations where you've had the most success. These characteristics should align with your product offerings, service levels, and ability to deliver value. Below are the most common factors to consider when identifying your target market profile (though please feel free to consider others that might be relevant to you).

1. Industry or sector

Which industries or sectors do you serve best? Look at the verticals where your solution aligns naturally with industry needs or challenges. Certain sectors may have specific requirements that your product or service meets particularly well.

- Example: If you specialise in supply chain optimisation software, industries like manufacturing, logistics, or retail may be in your "sweet spot". By narrowing your focus to industries where you already have experience or where your offering provides the most value, you improve your credibility and understanding of their needs.

2. Company size

The size of an organisation, based on revenue, employee count, or number of locations can significantly impact whether they are a good fit for your offering. Your solution may work better for small and mid-sized enterprises (SMEs) or may be specifically tailored for larger corporate of public sector enterprises. Things to consider include:

- Small businesses may have faster decision-making, simpler buying processes, but may also have smaller budgets and fewer internal resources.
- Mid-sized businesses may offer a better balance of agility and resources, and often have growth needs.
- Large enterprises usually have bigger budgets, greater resources, more complex procurement processes and longer decision-making cycles.

Ask yourself: What size organizations do you typically succeed with? Does your solution require scale, or is it ideal for smaller, flexible businesses?

3. Geographic location

Consider where your ideal customers are located. Are you focusing on specific regions, cities, or countries? Geography might play a role if you offer services that are location-dependent, or if certain areas align with your capacity to deliver. Things to consider include:

- A technology provider might focus on areas with a high concentration of tech-driven businesses, known as an area of community of interest.
- A logistics company might target regions with high manufacturing output, where demand for supply chain services is constant, ensuring a steady stream of potential clients.
- A renewable energy provider might focus on states or countries with favourable policies for green initiatives, such as tax incentives or government-backed sustainability programs, where businesses are more likely to invest in clean energy solutions.

Consider where you've had the most success so far. Align your target market profile with regions where demand, logistics, and budgets are in your favour.

4. Cultural fit and values

Cultural alignment matters more than many salespeople realise, especially in B2B. Businesses prefer to work with partners whose values, ethos and ways of working align with their own. Things to consider include:

- If your organisation values innovation and agility, you might prioritise working with companies that foster a culture of embracing new technologies and are open to rapid, iterative improvements
- If your company emphasises sustainability, you may find greater success selling to organisations with a similar commitment to green practices
- If your business prides itself on customer-centric service, targeting prospects that prioritise building deep, collaborative relationships with their own customers can create stronger mutual synergies.

Think about the type of customer you enjoy working with, companies that share your standards of professionalism, communication and approach to business challenges. When cultural fit exists, trust builds faster, relationships last longer and working together becomes more collaborative and productive.

5. Business challenges and needs

Focus on the problems or challenges your solution addresses. What specific needs or pain points does your ideal customer face? If you've done your research and qualification, you'll see patterns in the types of challenges you address repeatedly. Things to consider include:

- If your solution streamlines complex workflows, target businesses struggling with inefficiencies in operations or managing multiple disconnected systems. These organisations are more likely to benefit from, and invest in, process optimisation tools.
- If your product improves data security, prioritise businesses in highly regulated industries, like healthcare or finance, that face strict compliance challenges and need robust cybersecurity measures.
- If your service enhances customer engagement and retention, focus on companies with high customer churn rates or those looking to revamp their customer experience strategy to stay competitive.

By identifying businesses that share these needs, you're naturally aligning your solution with their challenges. Always remember, prospects want to buy solutions to their problems, not your products. The more closely their challenges match what you solve, the easier it becomes to communicate value and secure the deal.

6. Financial stability

Financial stability is an often overlooked but critical factor when defining your ideal customer target market profile. A company might align with all other characteristics, but if they can't afford your solution or are facing significant financial challenges, the likelihood of closing and maintaining a successful partnership diminishes. Things to consider include:

- Can they raise a budget for your product or service?
- Do they have a history of reliable partnerships and timely payments?
- Are they positioned for growth and therefore likely to invest in long-term solutions?

Choosing financially stable prospects minimizes the risk of deals falling apart due to budget constraints or internal issues.

If they ever answer the question of "what other suppliers are you considering" with "nobody", be careful that it's not because no one else will deal with them.

Bringing it all together

To define your ideal customer target market profile (your "sweet spot"), combine the five or six key characteristics that best represent your ideal B2B customer organisation. For example…

1. Industry: Mid-sized manufacturing companies.
2. Company size: 200–1,000 employees.
3. Geography: UK-based with a presence in metropolitan areas.
4. Challenges: Struggling with inefficient supply chain processes.
5. Cultural fit: Innovation-focused organizations seeking growth.
6. Financial stability: Growing businesses with budgets for process improvement solutions.

Once you've defined this profile, you'll have a clear and practical tool for evaluating prospects and ensuring they align with your ideal customer type.

The perils of ignoring your ideal customer target market profile

Failing to focus on your "sweet spot" can result in wasted resources, frustration, and a lot of dead-end opportunities. Here's what happens when you don't identify and stick to your target market profile.

1. Low win rates: Chasing prospects that aren't a good fit leads to prolonged sales cycles and fewer closed deals.
2. Resource drain: Time and energy spent on the wrong prospects could be better used elsewhere.
3. Misaligned solutions: Selling to organisations that don't have the problems you solve can damage your reputation if the solution doesn't deliver value.
4. Customer churn: A poor fit can lead to dissatisfied customers who are unlikely to stay loyal or grow with your business.

Focusing on your ideal customer saves time, improves efficiency and increases your success rate.

Exercise: Identifying your ideal customer target market profile

Objective: To define your ideal customer target market profile by identifying the specific characteristics of organisations most likely to benefit from your offerings.

Step 1: Evaluate your current and past successes

List four or five organisations you've successfully worked with in the past. For each, note the following.

1. Industry or sector: What industry were they in?
2. Company size: What was their size (revenue, employee count, physical locations)?
3. Geographic location: Where were they based?
4. Challenges: What specific problems or pain points did they face?
5. Cultural fit: Did they align with your company's values or way of working?
6. Financial stability: Were they financially stable and capable of investing in your solution?

Step 2: Identify patterns

Review the data from Step 1 to identify recurring characteristics. Ask yourself:

1. Are there common industries or sectors?
2. Do you see a pattern in company size or location?
3. What types of challenges do these organisations tend to face?
4. Are there similarities in their cultural values or operational style?
5. Were all these organisations financially stable?

Step 3: Define your ideal customer target market profile

Combine the recurring characteristics into a single profile. Use the following template:

1. Industry or Sector
2. Company Size
3. Geographic Location
4. Common Challenges
5. Cultural Fit
6. Financial Stability

Step 4: Practice

Using your "sweet spot" profile, evaluate a current or hypothetical prospect. For each characteristic, ask:

- Does the prospect match my ideal industry, size, location, etc.?

- Are their challenges aligned with the problems my solution solves and do I have proof of capability?
- Do they fit culturally with my company's values?
- Are they financially capable of investing in my offering?

If they align closely, they're a strong fit. If not, consider whether they're worth pursuing or if your time is better spent elsewhere.

Practice makes perfect

Reflect on your findings using the following prompts:

1. **Clarity**: How clear is your ideal customer target market profile? Does it focus on the most relevant characteristics?
2. **Alignment**: Did the prospect align with your ideal profile? If not, why?
3. **Next Steps**: What adjustments can you make to refine your ideal profile or improve your prospecting process?

Chapter 8: Prospecting

"Every contact you have with a prospect is an opportunity to build trust or destroy it." – Jill Konrath

Prospecting for new business is one of the most critical skills a B2B salesperson can develop, and every salesperson should know how to do it. While managing existing accounts is essential, securing new opportunities from within and outside your account base is what fuels growth, opens new markets and keeps your sales pipeline healthy. Without consistent prospecting efforts, even the most talented salesperson will eventually see their pipeline (and therefore results) dry up.

In this chapter, we'll explore the importance of prospecting, the challenges it presents and best practices to help you become a proficient B2B sales prospector.

Five reasons why prospecting matters.

1. Sustaining your sales pipeline: A healthy pipeline ensures you have enough opportunities at various stages of the sales cycle to meet or exceed your targets. Prospecting fills the top of the funnel, creating a steady flow of potential customers to nurture and close.

2. Achieving growth targets: Many companies set ambitious revenue goals and much of this growth comes from acquiring new customers. Effective prospecting ensures that you're contributing to your organisation's expansion and enhancing your personal profile.

3. Reducing reliance on existing customers: Over-reliance on existing accounts can leave you vulnerable if key customers reduce spending or move to competitors. Prospecting diversifies your portfolio, mitigating risk.

4. Building market presence: Regular and consistent prospecting positions you as a prominent and engaged participant within your market and customer base. By actively reaching out and addressing customer challenges, you cultivate a reputation as a reliable problem-solver, which can attract more inbound opportunities over time.

5. Engaging early: Proactive prospecting keeps you ahead of competitors by helping you to engage with potential customers before others do. By identifying and addressing prospects' needs early, you position yourself as a trusted partner, making it harder for competitors to gain a foothold. Don't rely on your prospect base to tell you what's going on in their business; be proactive and ask them.

Five challenges of prospecting

Prospecting can be intimidating, time-consuming and it often involves facing rejection. I don't think I've ever worked with a salesperson who actually loved prospecting or looked forward to doing it. Here are five common obstacles I've seen even the best salespeople encounter.

1. Finding the right prospects: Identifying ideal prospects can be challenging without a clear strategy. That's why establishing your ideal customer target market profile is such an important first step. Without this foundation, you may waste time chasing unqualified leads and pursuing opportunities that are unlikely to convert.

2. Overcoming fear of rejection: Many prospects are wary of cold approach or sales pitches, because of thoughts of dismissal and rejection. Even experienced salespeople can find it difficult to face frequent rejection, which can be demotivating and mentally exhausting. Finding creative and respectful ways to connect is essential to overcome this challenge.

3. Maintaining consistency: The daily grind of prospecting can feel repetitive and unrewarding, making it easy to deprioritise. Many salespeople fall into the trap of procrastination, spending more time thinking about prospecting than actually doing it. A structured schedule and disciplined approach are critical to staying on track.

4. Navigating complex decision-making structures: In B2B sales, prospects often operate within organisations with complex decision-making processes involving multiple stakeholders. Identifying the right contacts and understanding the decision-making hierarchy can be both time-consuming and challenging. However to get the maximum return on your efforts this needs to be done before you make contact. In my own personal experience, LinkedIn is a gold mine for this information. When I started out in the 1980s, the best information on offer was a hard copy of the "Kompass Guide" at the local library (ask your granddad, if he was in sales).

5. Balancing prospecting with other responsibilities: Salespeople more often than not have to juggle numerous tasks, from managing existing accounts to closing deals and everything in between. Prospecting can sometimes take a backseat to more immediate priorities, leading to inconsistent effort and a pipeline that eventually dries up.

Overcoming these challenges requires a robust plan, discipline and a commitment to continually refresh your sales pipeline. By addressing these obstacles head-on, salespeople can make prospecting a more productive and less daunting part of their routine.

Eight best practices for effective prospecting

1. Define your target market profile: As already mentioned, understanding who you're targeting is the foundation of successful prospecting. Before you begin your prospecting activity you need to know the following as a minimum. See chapter 7 for more on this.

2. Use multiple contact channels: Modern prospecting is thankfully no longer limited cold telephone calls. Today's salespeople are blessed with at least five channels to reach prospects. Here are some tips on how to leverage them effectively:

a) Phone: Despite the rise of digital communication, the phone still remains one of the most effective tools for initial contact outreach. A phone call allows you to create a personal connection and immediately convey your enthusiasm and expertise.

Best practices

- Begin with a strong opening statement that introduces who you are, the purpose of your call and why you believe your solution could add value to the prospect's business.
- Prepare by researching the prospect beforehand to tailor your conversation. This must be done before you make a call.
- Actively listen and engage with their responses to foster rapport and uncover insights.

Note: in the chapter annex I've provided 10 outline scripts for cold and warm calling and a referral outreach email template to help you help you on your way.

b) Email

Email is a cornerstone of modern prospecting, offering a scalable and non-intrusive way to connect. However, the key to success lies in personalisation and relevance, not in a scattergun approach of blasting out hundreds of unsolicited messages with a misplaced message. Again, use proof statements and referrals in subject lines and content whenever possible.

Best practices

- Craft personalised messages tailored to the recipient's specific needs, industry or pain points.
- Use compelling subject lines to grab attention and encourage the recipient to open the email.
- Include a clear and actionable call-to-action (for example, scheduling a meeting or reviewing a resource).

c) Social Media

LinkedIn and other platforms have transformed prospecting by providing opportunities to engage with prospects directly in a professional and less formal context. Social media allows you to establish credibility and build relationships and rapport over time, when used wisely.

Best practices

- Optimise your online profile to reflect your expertise and build trust with potential connections.
- Engage meaningfully by commenting on posts, sharing relevant content, and initiating conversations. Don't go straight into pitching your offer on first contact.
- Use tools like LinkedIn's advanced search and InMail to identify and reach decision-makers. This is sometimes funded by your company but can also be a worthwhile personal investment.

d) Networking events

Whether in-person or virtual, networking events offer excellent opportunities to connect with future prospects and build relationships in a more relaxed and collaborative environment.

Best practices

- Research attendees beforehand to identify key prospects and prepare conversation starters.
- Have an elevator pitch ready that succinctly explains who you are and what value you add to your customers, not what you do. Prospects are interested in what value you bring to them, not what your job title is.
- Contact people you would like to meet before the event and set up a conversation.

- Follow up promptly after the event with personalised messages to keep the conversation alive.

e) Video messages

In the digital world, video messages (either personalised one-to-one or for broadcast to a target group) can break through the noise and create a memorable impression. By addressing the prospect directly and tailoring your message, you show genuine effort and creativity.

Best practices

- Make the video engaging by using a conversational tone and showcasing enthusiasm for the value you add.
- Reference specific details about the prospect, their company or their market to make the message relevant.
- End with a clear call-to-action, such as scheduling a call or meeting to follow up.

3. Focus on personalisation

Generic messages are easily ignored. Tailoring your outreach to address the prospect's specific needs and challenges dramatically increases your chances of engagement.

Best practices

- Reference a mutual connection or shared interest.
- Highlight recent news about their company (for example, a new product launch or expansion).
- Show that you understand their industry and challenges.

Instead of saying, *"We provide solutions to help businesses improve efficiency,"* say:
"I noticed your company recently expanded into a new vertical market. Many of our clients in similar industries have found our supply chain solutions invaluable this arena." Make it about them, not you.

4. Use a proven framework

Prospecting frameworks provide structure and consistency. One popular approach is the AIDA model, famously referenced in the stage play and film "*Glengarry Glen Ross*" (a must-watch for any salesperson).

- Attention: Grab their attention with a compelling opening.
- Interest: Spark curiosity by addressing a key pain point or opportunity.
- Desire: Highlight the benefits of engaging with you.
- Action: End with a clear call to action, such as scheduling a meeting or call.

5. Seek referrals from existing customers

Someone once told me that "cold calling was God's punishment for salespeople who did not ask for referrals" and I think they're right!

Referrals from satisfied customers is the single most effective way to generate new business. A referral often comes with built-in trust, as it's based on the recommendation of someone the prospect already knows and respects.

Best practices

- Choose the right moment: Timing is critical. Ask for referrals from customers after delivering a positive result or receiving praise from them.
- Be specific: Don't just ask, *"Do you know anyone who could use our services?"* Instead, ask, *"Do you know anyone in your network facing similar challenges we've solved for you and would you introduce me to them?"*
- Make it easy: Offer to draft an introduction email or LinkedIn message they can forward.

Track your referrals and follow up promptly. Always thank your customer for the referral, regardless of the outcome.

6. Manage your time effectively

Effective time management is critical for maintaining consistent prospecting efforts and achieving long-term success. Without structure, prospecting can (and probably will) be deprioritised amidst other responsibilities.

Best practices

- Dedicate specific blocks of time each day, week or month to prospecting activities and stick to them without interruptions.
- Break tasks into focused intervals using techniques like the Pomodoro method* to maintain productivity and prevent burnout.
- Prioritise your outreach list to ensure you're consistently engaging with high-value prospects first.

*The Pomodoro method is a time management technique that boosts focus and productivity. It involves breaking work into 25-minute intervals called "Pomodoros" followed by 5-minute breaks. After completing four Pomodoros, take a longer 15–30 minute break. This method helps maintain concentration, prevent burnout and enhance task completion efficiency.

7. Quality not quantity

Effective prospecting isn't about volume, it's about quality. Qualifying prospects early ensures you focus your efforts on those most likely to convert. Check your qualification criteria and questions before you make contact.

Best practices

- Does the prospect have a genuine need for your solution?
- Do they have the budget to invest?
- Are you speaking with someone who has (or can connect you to) decision-making authority?

8. Integrate your channels

The value of utilising multiple channels lies in integration. No single channel operates in isolation, and combining various methods ensures you maximise engagement and reach opportunities.

Best practices

- Use complementary channels to reinforce your messaging; for example, follow up a phone call with a personalised email or a LinkedIn message.

- Adapt your approach based on where the prospect is most active to ensure your communication is relevant and timely.
- Maintain a consistent, value-driven message strategy and tone of voice across all channels to create a cohesive strategy.

Bringing it all together

Prospecting is the foundation of a successful B2B sales career. It's a skill that requires discipline, creativity and resilience. By defining your target customer, using a multi-channel approach and maintaining a consistent effort, you can fill your pipeline with high-quality opportunities and set yourself up for long-term success.

Remember, prospecting isn't just about finding new leads; it's about building relationships, solving problems, and creating value. When done well, it transforms cold calls into meaningful conversations and strangers into loyal customers.

Don't neglect referrals. They're the gold standard of prospecting. By making the most of the trust and satisfaction of your existing customers, you can reduce the time and effort needed to build credibility with new prospects. On the page that follows is an example of the email format I use when I have gained a referral from an existing customer.

Exercise: Building a prospecting plan

Objective: To create a simple, actionable prospecting plan using your ideal customer target market profile and implement two to three specific outreach steps.

Step 1: Build your prospecting plan

Using your ideal customer profile, define the following key elements:

1. Target industry: What industries or sectors are you focusing on?
   Example: Manufacturing or logistics.
2. Company size: What is the typical size of your ideal customer (number of employees, revenue)?
   Example: Mid-sized companies with 200–500 employees.
3. Key decision-makers: Who are the primary contacts you need to reach?
   Example: Operations managers, procurement heads, or sales directors.
4. Common pain points: What challenges or problems do your prospects typically face that your solution can address or what do you know about that specific prospect's

challenges?

Example: Inefficient supply chain processes or rising operational costs.

Step 2: Identify your outreach channels

Select one or more channels for reaching your prospects effectively. The channels should align with where your prospects are most likely to engage.

- Phone: For direct, personal outreach.
- Email: For scalable, personalised communication.
- LinkedIn: For professional, relationship-driven interactions.

Step 3: Implement two to three simple steps

Choose and execute two or three specific actions from the following list and apply each to at least 10 organisations in your prospect list.

Cold call:

- Research the prospect to identify a relevant challenge or opportunity
- Prepare a 30-second introduction that explains who you are, why you're calling, and how you can help
- Sample script:
  "Hi [Name], this is [Your Name] from [Company]. I noticed your team recently expanded operations, and many of our clients in similar industries have found our [solution] helpful in managing [specific challenge]. Can I take a few minutes of your time to explain how we can help or would it make sense to discuss this further at another time?"

Personalised Email:

Use the AIDA framework:

- **Attention**: Write a compelling subject line (e.g., "Solutions for streamlining your supply chain").
- **Interest**: Reference a challenge specific to their industry.
- **Desire**: Highlight how your solution has helped similar companies.
- **Action**: Ask for a brief meeting or call.

- Sample email:

   "Hi [Name],

   I noticed your company has been growing in [specific area]. Many of our clients in similar industries have found our [solution] invaluable for [specific benefit]. I'd love to explore how we can help your team achieve similar results. Would you be open to a call in the coming days?"

   Best regards,

   [Your Name]"

LinkedIn connection request:

- Send a connection request with a personalised message.
- Sample script:

   "Hi [Name], I came across your profile and noticed your work in [industry/role]. I'd love to connect and share how we've been helping companies like [their company name] address [specific challenge]. Looking forward to connecting."

Practice makes perfect

After implementing your plan, reflect on the following and take actions for improvement.

1. Which channel generated the most engagement?
2. Did your messaging resonate with prospects?
3. What can you improve in your next round of outreach?

Ensure you follow up promptly with any prospect who shows interest to keep the momentum going.

Chapter 8, annex: telephone call scripts and referral email

"The more you sweat in practice, the less you bleed in battle." – Richard Marciano.

As mentioned earlier, outbound calls remain a vital component of effective prospecting, offering an opportunity to engage prospects directly and personally. However, success requires preparation, strategy and the right approach.

In this section I'll share 10 examples of call scripts tailored for different prospecting scenarios, from initial contact to leveraging referrals. Each script is designed to help you connect meaningfully, address specific challenges and guide prospects toward the next step in your sales process.

These scripts are a combination of techniques I have been trained in, authority articles I have encountered and best practices of colleagues I have witnessed.

1. The first approach call

"Hi [prospect's name], this is [Your Name] from [Your Company Name]".

"I've been learning about (Prospect's Company Name) and noticed (specific challenge or opportunity related to their role or business or market). At (Your Company Name), we specialise in helping businesses like yours with (Value Proposition 1, Value Proposition 2, Value Proposition 3)".

"Does this sound like something that might help with (identified specific challenges)"?

Outcome: If the response is positive…

"Brilliant, could we schedule a time for a longer conversation or short presentation to explore how we can help. What does your schedule look like this week?"

Outcome: If the response is less positive

"I understand. Would it be okay if I sent you a follow-up email with some information and resources? I'll follow up tomorrow/next week so we can discuss further".

2. The gatekeeper call

Gatekeepers, such as personal assistants and departmental managers, often screen calls for decision-makers. They can be an obstacle or a helpful ally, depending on how you approach the interaction. Always remain professional and polite while explaining the purpose of your call.

Example

"Hi, I'm calling for (Prospect's Name). This is (Your Name] with (Your Company Name).".

Outcome: If the gatekeeper transfers you to the prospect (if you're lucky)

"Thank you", then proceed with your pre-prepared call script.

Outcome: When questioned about the purpose of the call

"I'm following up on (specific reason; an email, previous contact or reference to something the target prospect might have posted on-line). Could you let them know I'd like to connect? If not, I'd be happy to leave a voicemail".

A word of warning on gatekeeper calls: never tell lies to get through the gate. You may come across sales trainers who advise you to claim you know the contact (when you don't) or that they are expecting your call (when they're not). These tactics might get you connected on a call, but you will have fallen at the first fence when it comes to trust. It's a stupid thing to do.

3. Qualification call

Qualification calls are intended to better understand your prospect's challenges and qualify them as a potential customer. This is your chance to ask thoughtful questions and gather insights to tailor your approach.

Example

"Hi (Prospect's Name), this is (Your Name] from [Your Company Name)".

"I've been learning about (Prospect's Company Name) and wanted to ask a few questions about [specific challenges or opportunities)" that I genuinely believe I could help you with."

Potential follow-on questions:

- *"Are you experiencing challenges with [specific problem]? If so, what are they?"*

- *"What steps have you taken to address these challenges?"*
- *"Are there any roadblocks preventing you from finding a better solution?"*
- *"What does your ideal solution look like?"*

Outcome: If the response is positive:

"Thank you for sharing that information. I believe [Your Company Name] can help. Can we set up a time to discuss this further/arrange a short presentation/a deeper discussion/short presentation?"

Outcome: If the response is less positive:

"Thanks for your guidance, I understand. Would it be okay if I followed up with some additional information? I'll reach out tomorrow/next week/ next month to check in with you to see if you feel there's value in exploring further"?

4. Recommended and referred by a mutual contact

When you're referred by someone the prospect knows, it builds immediate credibility. Use the recommendation to establish rapport and set the tone for the conversation.

Example

"Hi (Prospect's Name), this is (Your Name) from (Your Company Name)".

"(Mutual Contact's Name) recommended I connect with you. I've been learning about (Prospect's Company Name) and wanted to discuss how we help businesses like yours with (specific value propositions").

"Do you have a few minutes now or would another time work better"?

Outcome: If the response is positive:

"That's great! I'd love to dive deeper into how we can assist. What time works best for a more detailed conversation?"

Outcome: If the response is negative:

"I understand. Would it be okay if I sent you a follow-up email with some additional information? I can reach out later to see if it aligns with your priorities?"

5. Asking for a direct connection to a decision-maker

If you're struggling to reach a decision-maker, try asking another team member for an introduction. They may also provide valuable context about the company. Contacts who fall into this category can also help guide your through the prospects decision-making process

Example

Hi (Referrer's Name]) this is (Your Name) from (Your Company Name".

"I've been trying to connect with (Prospect's Name) but haven't had any luck. Could you help by introducing me via email / at a specified event, etc? We specialise in helping companies like (Prospect's Company Name) with (Value Proposition 1, Value Proposition 2, Value Proposition 3)".

Outcome: If the response is positive:

"Thank you so much for helping facilitate this connection. I'll follow up with an email containing all the relevant information. Let me know if there's anything else you need from me."

Outcome: If the response is less positive:

"I understand. Is there someone else in the organisation you think might be a better point of contact? Alternatively, would it be okay if I followed up with you in the future if circumstances change?"

6. Following up

A follow-up call lets your prospect know you're serious about connecting. Reference your previous outreach to maintain consistency.

Example

"Hi (Prospect's Name), this is (Your Name) from (Your Company Name).

"Did you have a chance to review the email I sent about [specific topic or solution]? I'd love to hear your thoughts".

Outcome: If the response is positive:

"Brilliant, do you have time now to explore further or would it work better for you for us to schedule a time to dive deeper into how we can help. What works best for you?"

Outcome: If the response is less positive:

"No problem. Can I resend the email and follow up again at a more convenient time for you?

7. Special promotion call

A promotional offer can make your outreach more compelling (as long as whatever it is your offering is of relevance and value to the prospect). Highlight the value and urgency of your promotion to encourage action.

Example

"Hi "Prospect's Name", this is (Your Name) from (Your Company Name)".

"We're currently offering ([specific promotion). I'd love to help you take advantage of this opportunity to address [specific challenges or objectives]".

Does this sound like something that could be valuable to you and would you like to hear more?"

Outcome: If the response is positive:

"That's fantastic! Let's discuss how we can make the most of this offer for you. Do you have time now for us to go over the details or would you like to set up a meeting to explore it in more depth"?

Outcome: If the response is less positive:

"I completely understand. Could I send you some additional information about the promotion in case it aligns with future priorities? I'd be happy to follow up if your requirements change".

8. Previously spoke with the prospect's colleague

If a previous contact has left the company or handed off the conversation, continue where it left off. You won't believe how often this has happened to me in the last 40 years (I don't take it personally though).

Example

"Hi (Prospect's Name), this is (Your Name) from [Your Company Name)".

"I previously spoke with (former contact's name) about (specific challenge or opportunity) and wanted to follow up with you to continue the conversation".

Outcome: If the response is positive:

"That's great thank you. I'd love to bring you up to speed and explore how we can move forward. Is now convenient or would you prefer a meeting or call at a more convenient time for you"?

Outcome: If the response is less positive:

"I fully understand. Is there someone else in your organisation who might be better positioned to discuss this with me? Alternatively, would it be okay if I followed up at a better time with you"?

9. Establishing a 1:1 connection

Building rapport on a personal level can create a more relaxed and engaging conversation.

Example

"Hi (Prospect's Name), this is (your name]) from (your company name).

"I noticed your recent post about (specific topic) and found it really compelling. It's exactly why I wanted to connect to learn more about (Prospect's Company Name) objectives and challenges."

Outcome: If the response is positive

"Thanks for taking the time. I'd love to learn more about your goals and explore how we can support you. What's a good time for us to have a more detailed discussion?"

Outcome: If the response is less positive

"I understand. Perhaps I could I share some insights or resources? I'd be happy to follow up in the future when the timing works better for you."

10. Contact regarding a company success

Acknowledging a company milestone shows that you're paying attention and can position your solution as timely and relevant.

Example

"Hi (Prospect's Name), this is (your name] from [your company name]"

"Congratulations on (specific company achievement). I know times like this often bring new opportunities and challenges. I'd love to discuss how we can help with (specific challenges or goals)".

For all outcomes use the first approach call responses as follows.

Outcome: If the response is positive

"Brilliant, could we schedule a time for a deeper conversation or short presentation to explore how we can help. What does your schedule look like this week"?

Outcome: If the response is less positive

"I understand. Would it be okay if I sent you a follow-up email with some information and resources? I'll follow up tomorrow/next week so we can discuss further".

Referral email to new prospect

Below is an example of the email I send to new prospects when I have the agreement to use an existing customer as a referral. The key things to note are:

- Use the referrer's name and a reference to the value you bring in the subject line.
- Open with a simple one sentence introduction. A weak opening means the rest of the email won't be read.
- Limit the core section of your pitch, make it easy to understand what you can do for them (it's all about them, not about you).
- Finish with a clear call to action.
- Ensure the whole email is less than 150 words.
- After the email is sent, make sure you follow up exactly when you said you would.

To: anya@abcindustries.com

Subject: Anya; Rob Nowak suggested we talk about Improving ABC Industries network resilience by 40%

Hi Anya,

Rob Nowak (of XYZ ltd) suggested I get in touch with you to discuss helping you with your 2025 network resilience plans, like we've just done for him.

It would be great to have a conversation with you, especially if you would like to discuss the following areas,

- *Significantly increasing network resilience to physical and virtual intervention.*
- *Enhancing network resilience to cyber-attacks by over 70%.*
- *Reducing pro-rata network management costs, including flexible financing plans.*

These are all areas in which we have helped a number of organisations in your industry achieve significant improvements.

If you are looking at any of the above, it would be great to find out more about your plans. Can we arrange an initial call on Monday or Wednesday next week, or is there a time that suits you better?

Chapter 9: Preparing for customer meetings

"You might not win a £5m deal in a single meeting, but you can definitely lose it." - David Hughes.

In B2B sales, preparation is everything. A well-prepared meeting can be the turning point in the sales cycle, moving you closer to a deal and solidifying your value in the customer's eyes. On the other hand, a lack of preparation can not only damage your credibility but potentially cost you a valuable opportunity. While you may not be able to win a high-value deal in a single meeting, you can certainly lose one if you haven't done the groundwork.

In this chapter we'll explore the practical steps required to prepare effectively for customer meetings, ensuring you make the most of every opportunity and that the person who turns up is the best version of you.

By defining objectives, researching thoroughly and creating a collaborative agenda with the customer, you'll set yourself up for success.

Step 1: Know your customer inside and out

Preparation begins with research. Before you step into the meeting, you should have a solid understanding of your customer's business, their industry and the challenges they may be facing. This demonstrates professionalism, saves time, and shows the customer you are invested in their success. Practical steps for customer research include:

- Company overview: Learn the basics about their organisation, size, location, product offerings, market presence and any recent news or changes. Check their website, annual reports, press releases, and social media channels
- Industry trends: Understand what's happening in their sector. Are there any major challenges, disruptions or opportunities?
- Key decision-makers: Identify who will be attending the meeting. Learn about their roles, responsibilities, and priorities, LinkedIn is an excellent tool for this.
- Previous interactions: Review notes from prior conversations, emails, or meetings with the customer. Ensure you are clear on any commitments or follow-up items from previous discussions.

By investing time in understanding their world, you position yourself as a credible advisor rather than someone who's just trying to sell them something.

Step 2: Define your meeting objectives

Walking into a customer meeting without clear objectives is like setting out on a journey without a map. You need to know exactly what you want to achieve to make the meeting productive for both parties. The question to ask yourself is, *"why is this meeting taking place"?* Practical steps to define objectives include:

- Clarify your objectives. What do you hope to accomplish. Are you seeking to qualify a key business challenge the customer is facing. Are you looking to present your solution, or agree on next steps in the sales process? If you don't have a clear objective, you have no way of gauging the success (or otherwise) of the meeting.
- Qualify and deliver the customer's objectives: Think about what the customer may want to get out of the meeting. Their objectives will often differ from yours, so it's important to align early.
- Make sure you find out what the customer wants to achieve before you attend the meeting. Ask the customer in advance, *"what would a successful outcome of this meeting look like to you"?*

This question, simple as it is, immediately makes the meeting feel collaborative. It also ensures you're focused on what truly matters to the customer, preventing you from going off track.

Step 3: Plan the meeting agenda

A structured agenda helps keep the meeting focused, efficient and productive. A great meeting feels like a two-way conversation rather than a one-sided presentation. Steps for building the agenda include:

- Start with purpose: Communicate the purpose of the meeting upfront. For example, *"The aim of today's meeting is to better understand your priorities and discuss how our solution might help address some of your challenges."*
- Outline key topics: Break the meeting into clear, manageable sections, such as a brief review of your understanding of their needs; discussion or presentation of your proposed solution; time for feedback, questions, or objections; agreement on next steps.
- Ensure you include the customer's stated objectives in the agenda and never forget to ask if anything has changed before you proceed.

- Allow for flexibility: Build in time for open discussion. Meetings often take unexpected turns and that's okay; some of the most valuable insights come from unplanned conversations.
- Share the agenda: Send a brief outline of the agenda to the customer ahead of the meeting. This gives them a chance to prepare, signals that you value their time and gives them the opportunity to request edits and amendments.
- Check the time: This might seem an obvious point, but it is imperative that you confirm exactly how much time the customer has allocated to you. Without this knowledge you risk trying to pack too much into the agenda and derailing the meeting.

Step 4: Prepare the right questions

Good preparation includes thinking through the questions you want to ask during the meeting. Asking the right questions helps you uncover information, build rapport, and demonstrate a genuine interest in solving the customer's challenges. Practical steps for preparing questions include:

Focus on open-ended questions: These encourage the customer to share more than just "yes" or "no" answers. For example:

- What are the biggest challenges you're facing in this area right now?
- How is this challenge impacting your business operations or goals?

Align questions to your objectives: Use questions to gather the information you need to achieve your objectives for the meeting. If your objective is to confirm their pain points, focus on uncovering and validating those areas

Ask about success: Use my favourite question to set the tone early: *"What would make this a successful meeting for you?"* This helps clarify expectations and immediately shifts the conversation to what matters most to the customer. Even if you have covered this with them it's worthwhile asking again

Prepare follow-up questions: Be ready to dive deeper based on their answers. Probing questions like, *"can you expand on that?"* or *"what impact is that having?"* keep the conversation flowing and uncover valuable insights.

Step 5: Anticipate customer questions and objections

Preparation is not just about the questions you ask, it's also about anticipating what the customer may ask you. In B2B sales, customers are often well informed and their questions can be detailed and challenging. Prepare answers for the common customer questions.

These might include:

- How does your solution compare to that of your competitors?
- What kind of ROI can we expect?
- How long will implementation take?
- Do you have examples of this working for other companies like ours?

If you are attending the meeting with colleagues, agree beforehand who will answer which type of question and ensure you are aligned on your prepared answers.

Think through any concerns or objections the customer may raise and prepare thoughtful, honest responses. For example:

- If price is a common objection, be ready to articulate the value and ROI your solution delivers.

Be fully prepared to answer any questions about features, benefits, or functionality of your product or service. Anticipating questions allows you to respond with confidence, which builds trust and credibility. If it's going to be a technical meeting and your knowledge is not deep enough, take someone whose knowledge is.

Step 6: Qualifying attendees and handling unannounced participants

A key aspect of effective meeting preparation is qualifying in advance who from the customer's organisation will be attending. Understanding the roles and responsibilities of participants helps you tailor the discussion to their specific interests and priorities. However, unannounced participants can sometimes show up, requiring adaptability during the meeting. Here's how to handle both situations effectively.

Qualify Attendees in Advance:

- Before the meeting, confirm with the customer who will be attending. Ask for the names, roles, and job titles of all participants. This helps you understand their potential concerns and the influence they may have on the decision-making process

- Use tools like LinkedIn to research attendees and prepare for their unique perspectives and questions.

Clarify their objectives

- Along with confirming attendees, ask about their objectives for the meeting. Ask, "*what does each participant hope to gain from this discussion*?" This ensures that you're prepared to address their specific needs and expectations.

Prepare for unannounced participants

Despite your best efforts, it's not uncommon for additional individuals to join the meeting without prior notice. When this happens:

- Politely acknowledge their presence and ask about their role in the organisation. For instance: "*It's great to have you join us, could you share a bit about your role and how we can address your priorities today*"?
- Be prepared to provide a brief recap of key points discussed earlier to bring them up to speed without derailing the agenda.
- Flexibly adjust the conversation to include their input while keeping the meeting's primary objectives on track.

Document and follow up

After the meeting, ensure you document the contributions and concerns of all participants, including those who joined unexpectedly. Follow up with personalised responses or materials addressing their specific points of interest. This shows professionalism and ensures they know that what's important to them is not overlooked.

By proactively qualifying attendees and skilfully handling unexpected participants, you maintain control of the meeting and demonstrate your ability to adapt, ensuring a productive and engaging discussion for all involved.

Step 7: Build rapport and establish credibility

Even with all the preparation in the world, if you fail to connect with the customer on a human level, the meeting will fall flat. Building rapport and establishing credibility are vital to creating a productive, positive meeting experience. Practical tips for building rapport include:

- Be professional and personable: Start the meeting with a friendly, genuine tone. Small talk can help break the ice but keep it relevant and brief.
- Demonstrate you've done your research: Mention a recent achievement, news story, or key fact about the customer's business. This shows you're prepared and genuinely interested in their success. For example: *"I saw that your company recently launched a new product line, congratulations. I'd love to hear how that's going for you"?*
- Be curious: Listen actively and ask thoughtful questions. Customers value salespeople who care about their challenges rather than just their own agenda.
- Be authentic: Avoid overly rehearsed or robotic interactions. Be yourself, and aim for an honest, consultative conversation. This is a key component in building trust.

Step 8: Prepare a meeting plan

As we have discussed, successful outcomes to customer meetings hinge on thorough preparation. A well-structured meeting plan not only sets the tone for a productive experience, it also ensures alignment among your team and creates a professional impression on your customer.

By sharing your meeting plan internally for input and feedback, you can harness your colleagues' expertise and foster collaboration to achieve better outcomes. The benefits of preparing and sharing a meeting plan include:

- Clear objectives and focus: A meeting plan outlines primary objectives, helping your team to stay on track. With defined objectives, you can prioritise key topics, ensuring the meeting is both efficient and productive.
- Enhanced collaboration and input: Sharing your meeting plan internally allows colleagues to review and contribute their insights, ensuring all perspectives are considered. This collaborative approach can uncover blind spots, refine strategies, and result in a more robust agenda.
- Preparedness and professionalism: A detailed meeting plan helps your team prepare thoroughly, anticipate potential customer questions, and align their messaging. This level of preparation demonstrates professionalism and builds trust with your B2B customers.
- Effective role allocation: When your team understands the meeting's agenda and objectives in advance, roles and responsibilities can be clearly defined. This ensures that everyone knows their part, avoids duplication of efforts, and fosters a cohesive team dynamic during the meeting

- Stronger team confidence: Internal feedback on the plan empowers your team to feel confident about the meeting strategy. When colleagues feel their voices are heard and their expertise valued, they are more likely to engage positively during the discussion.

A copy of the johnpc ltd customer meeting planner can be found at the end of this chapter.

Step 9: The final checklist: your pre-meeting preparation

Before heading into the meeting, take a moment to run through this quick checklist:

- Research completed: You know the company, their industry, and key decision-makers.
- Objectives defined: You're clear on what you want to achieve in the meeting.
- Questions prepared: You've outlined key questions to uncover needs and priorities.
- Customer objectives clarified: You've asked, *"what would make this a successful meeting for you?"*
- Agenda outlined: You have a structured plan for the meeting which you have shared with the customer.
- Anticipated questions: You're ready to answer the customer's likely queries or objections.

Preparation Builds Confidence and Trust

Preparing for a customer meeting is not administration or merely about ticking boxes; it's about ensuring you show up as the best version of yourself, ready to deliver value.

Remember: The goal is to collaborate with the customer, not to pitch at them. When you open the meeting by asking, *"What would make this a successful meeting for you?"* you immediately signal that you're there to listen, understand, and solve their problems. Combine preparation with a genuine focus on the customer, and every meeting becomes an opportunity to move the sales process forward with confidence and trust.

Exercise: Preparing for customer meetings

Objective: To create a structured meeting preparation plan and implement key steps to ensure a productive and professional customer meeting.

Step 1: Build your meeting preparation plan

Use the following template to prepare for your customer meeting:

Customer Research:

- What is the company's size, industry and recent news?
- Who are the key contacts attending the meeting?
- What challenges or opportunities do they face in their industry?

Meeting Objectives:

- What do you want to achieve by the end of the meeting? (qualify challenges, present solutions, define next steps).
- What does the customer want to achieve? Ask in advance: "What would make this meeting successful for you?"

Agenda:

- Create a structured outline for the meeting.
- Start with introductions and purpose.
- Discuss key topics (e.g., challenges, solutions, Q&A).
- Conclude with clear next steps.
- Confirm how much time the customer has allocated for the meeting.

Step 2: Implement key preparation steps

Choose and complete 2-3 simple, actionable steps to ensure thorough preparation.

Research key attendees:

- Use LinkedIn to research their roles, priorities and any public activity.
- Prepare one personalised insight for each attendee, such as referencing a recent achievement, initiative or something they've posted online.

Prepare questions:

Develop three or four open-ended questions aligned with your meeting objectives, such as:

- What are the biggest challenges your team is facing in this area?
- How are these challenges impacting your business operations or goals?
- What would success look like for your organisation after addressing these challenges?

Anticipate questions and objections:

- Think of two or three likely questions the customer might ask (e.g., ROI, timelines, competitor comparisons) and prepare concise, confident responses.

Step 3: Practice section

Choose one of the following scenarios to apply your preparation plan:

Scenario A: Meeting with a mid-sized logistics company to discuss inefficiencies in their supply chain.

Scenario B: Presenting to a large financial institution about improving their cybersecurity measures.

Scenario C: A first meeting with a growing tech startup exploring customer retention solutions.

Practice

- Outline the agenda and objectives for the meeting.
- Draft two or three personalised questions and one prepared response to a potential customer question or objection.

Practice makes perfect

After preparing or conducting your meeting, reflect on the following:

Preparation quality: Did your research and planning adequately address the customer's needs and priorities?

Customer engagement: Were your questions effective in uncovering key insights and fostering a collaborative discussion?

Next steps: What actions do you need to take to build on the outcomes of the meeting?

Chapter 10: Qualification, qualification, qualification

"It ain't what we don't know that gets us into trouble, it's what we know for sure that just ain't so." - Mark Twain.

Sales as an art and a science is nowhere more apparent than in the qualification of high-value, complex opportunities involving multiple decision-makers.

In these opportunities robust qualification is the cornerstone of success. Without a rigorous qualification process, salespeople risk wasting resources chasing opportunities that are unlikely to close or failing to uncover the full potential of promising leads.

As we have already touched on, high-value, complex sales are fundamentally different from transactional sales. They involve lengthy sales cycles, intricate buyer needs, significant financial investments, and multiple stakeholders. These characteristics make qualification both more challenging and more critical. Effective qualification ensures that sales teams focus their efforts on opportunities with the highest likelihood of success, optimising resource allocation and improving win rates.

In these scenarios, robust qualification is not a one-time event but a continuous process. It requires consistent evaluation and alignment with the customer's needs, timelines and the decision-making process. A failure to qualify robustly can lead to overconfidence in weak opportunities or missed signals from strong ones.

In this chapter we'll explore how robust qualification processes underpin success in complex sales, and provide actionable strategies to navigate them.

A tale of two opportunities

1. The forklift fumble

Early in my sales career at Crown Lift Trucks, I had what I thought was a golden opportunity to sell a forklift truck to a medium-sized logistics company. The customer seemed enthusiastic and I jumped headfirst into pitching the features and benefits of our product. I was confident. After all, who wouldn't want a top-of-the-line Crown forklift?

But as the weeks dragged on, cracks began to appear. Meetings were postponed, questions went unanswered and the decision-makers were mysteriously absent. I chalked it up to typical delays and pressed on, convinced the deal was just a signature away.

It wasn't until much later, after investing countless hours into demos, proposals and follow-ups, that I realised the hard truth. I was being used to benchmark prices and functionality against other competitors. Worse still, the decision-making power didn't lie with the enthusiastic manager I'd been working with, it rested with a finance director I had never met, who had already decided to go with another supplier before I'd even made my first call.

Looking back, it was a painful but invaluable lesson in the importance of robust qualification. Had I asked the right questions up front about budget, decision-makers, and compelling events, I could have saved myself weeks of wasted effort. Instead, I learned the hard way that hope is not a strategy.

2: The network triumph

Years later, while at Case Communications, I found myself in a high-stakes opportunity to sell a communications network to a multinational manufacturing company. This time, I approached the deal with the discipline of someone who had learned from past mistakes.

From the outset, I focused on qualification. I didn't just dive into pitching, I took the time to understand their pain points, their decision-making process, basis of decision and crucially, their compelling events. The IT director was my initial point of contact, but I knew he wasn't the sole decision-maker. Through careful questioning, I identified the CFO and the COO as key stakeholders and made sure to align my messaging with their priorities: cost efficiency for the CFO and operational reliability for the COO.

A pivotal moment came when I uncovered a compelling event; a major contract with one of their largest clients was contingent on upgrading their network. This gave the project a sense of urgency, which I used to keep the process moving forward.

By the time we reached the proposal stage, I had built relationships with all the key players, addressed potential objections, understood their resonating focus and ensured their budget aligned with our solution. The deal closed smoothly and on schedule and it was one of the most satisfying wins of my career, not just because of the revenue, but because it validated the planning and hard work I'd invested in robust qualification.

The pillars of effective qualification

To navigate the complexity of multi-decision-maker opportunities, sales people must adopt a structured approach to qualification. Below are seven key pillars that form the foundation of an effective qualification framework.

1. Understanding the customer's challenge

At the heart of any successful sales effort is a deep understanding of the customer's challenges. In complex sales, buyers are often motivated by strategic needs, such as cost savings, operational efficiency or competitive advantage. These pain points are usually intertwined with broader organisational goals. Start the qualification process by asking probing questions to uncover, such as:

- What problems are they trying to solve?
- Why are these problems critical now?
- What is the potential impact of solving these challenges?

When these pain points are clearly understood, salespeople can tailor their value propositions to resonate with the customer's priorities.

2. Identifying stakeholders and decision-makers

In high-value opportunities, the decision-making process often involves a committee of stakeholders with varying levels of influence and interest. Identifying these individuals and understanding their roles is a crucial aspect of qualification.

Key considerations include:

- Who holds the budget? Determine who controls the financial resources for the purchase.
- Who influences the decision? Look for individuals whose input will sway the buying decision.
- Who are the end users? Understand the perspectives of those who will use the product or service.
- Who can block the deal? Identify potential detractors and address their concerns early.

Mapping out the decision-making ecosystem allows salespeople to tailor their messaging to each stakeholder's priorities and objections.

3. Evaluating the budget

A common pitfall in complex sales is pursuing opportunities where the budget is misaligned with the solution's cost. Early in the qualification process, it's essential to assess whether the customer has allocated sufficient money and resources for the purchase.

Questions to explore include:

- Is there an approved budget for this initiative?
- If not, what is the process for obtaining budget approval?
- How does the budget compare to the perceived value of solving the problem?

Transparent discussions about budget demonstrate professionalism and ensure there are no surprises later in the sales process.

4. Establishing the compelling events

Complex opportunities often suffer from prolonged or undefined timelines. Without a clear sense of urgency, opportunities can stagnate. Understanding the customer's timeline is critical for prioritising efforts and forecasting revenue. It's important to establish:

- What is the desired implementation date?
- Are there external deadlines driving this initiative?
- What happens if the timeline slips? (This is a killer question and must always be asked).

A well-defined timeline not only helps with internal planning but also provides leverage for keeping the sales process on track.

5. Assessing fit and feasibility

Not every prospect is a good fit for your solution. Qualification involves an honest evaluation of whether your product or service aligns with the customer's needs, constraints and expectations. Key areas to explore include:

- Does your solution address their core challenges?
- Are there technical or operational barriers to implementation?
- Is the customer culturally aligned with the way your company delivers value?

Being upfront about potential mismatches builds trust and preserves long-term relationships.

6. Understanding the decision-making process

In multi-decision-maker environments, understanding how decisions are made is just as important as knowing who makes them. Each organisation will have a unique process, and navigating it effectively requires insight and adaptability. Questions to clarify include,

- What are the formal steps in the decision-making process?
- Are there informal influencers who shape decisions?
- What criteria will be used to evaluate potential vendors?
- How does procurement fit into the process?

Gaining this clarity early allows sales teams to align their efforts with the customer's process and avoid unnecessary delays.

7. Qualifying continuously

Qualification is not a one-and-done activity. Throughout the sales cycle, new information emerges that may alter the opportunity's viability. Regularly revisiting qualification criteria ensures that the deal remains worth pursuing. Look for red flags such as,

- Shifts in the customer's priorities or budget
- Resistance to providing necessary information
- Changes in key stakeholders

Continuous qualification enables sales teams to pivot or disengage early, minimising wasted effort.

Qualifying opportunities out as well as in

An essential but often overlooked aspect of qualification is knowing when to disqualify an opportunity. Not all leads are worth pursuing, and focusing on the wrong ones can drain valuable time and resources. Qualifying opportunities out ensures that sales teams concentrate on deals with a genuine chance of success.

As an ex-colleague of mine, Neil Gokcen, used to say, *"If you're going to lose, lose early and make it your decision."* There's nothing worse than wasting time, money and emotions on opportunities you're never going to win. Salespeople who fail to learn this lesson will eventually suffer from a lack of credibility with their colleagues and find it increasingly difficult to gain their support for future opportunities.

Signs an opportunity should be qualified out include:

- The customer's budget is significantly misaligned with the solution.
- There is no clear timeline or urgency to act.
- Stakeholders are unresponsive or unwilling to engage.
- The organisation is a poor match to your target market profile.
- The customer organisation lacks a clear need or motivation for change.
- Decision-makers are overly committed to a competitor.

How to approach qualifying out

Qualifying out an opportunity doesn't mean burning bridges. It should be done professionally and with empathy, leaving the door open for future engagement. Here are some best practices:

- Be transparent: Clearly explain why the opportunity isn't a good fit at this time.
- Offer alternatives: Suggest solutions or timelines that might work better for the customer.
- Stay in touch: Maintain a relationship through check-ins or by sharing relevant insights.

A tale of two qualifying out scenarios

1. **The opportunity that wouldn't end**

During my time at Case Communications, I had an opportunity that, in hindsight, I should have qualified out early. It started with a mid-sized financial services company that expressed interest in upgrading their communications network. On the surface, it looked promising, they had a growing need for bandwidth and seemed receptive to our solution.

But as the conversations progressed, the red flags started piling up. Budget approval kept getting pushed back, the IT team couldn't articulate a clear timeline and when I asked about the decision-making process, the answers were vague at best. Still, I convinced myself that persistence would pay off. I kept pushing forward, scheduling more meetings and revising proposals in the hope that clarity would emerge.

Weeks turned into months. The opportunity consumed countless hours of my time and energy, not to mention resources from my technical team. Eventually, I discovered the harsh truth. The company had no serious intention of moving forward. They were "window shopping", comparing vendors to build a negotiation argument for reduced costs from their existing supplier, who they had no intention of leaving.

Looking back, I can see where I went wrong. I ignored the signs, unclear budgets, no compelling event and a lack of engagement from key stakeholders. I became a victim of good news selling, convincing myself that all would come good. If I had qualified the opportunity out early, I could have redirected my efforts to higher-potential deals and saving myself the embarrassment of having to remove the opportunity from my forecast (after six months). Instead, I learned a hard lesson about the cost of clinging to a lost cause.

2. **Dodging a bullet at Lehman Brothers**

In 2008, one of my sales teams was approached by Lehman Brothers to bid on a large-scale structured cabling solution for a new facility they were planning in London. It was a high-value opportunity and at first glance, seemed like the kind of marquee project any salesperson would want to win. But something about the situation didn't sit right with me.

During the qualification process, I started pushing the team to dig deeper, which they were nervous of doing due to the size of the opportunity and (their perceived) status of the prospect.

Lehman's timelines for implementation were unusually aggressive, and when I inquired about budget allocation, the answers were surprisingly non-committal for a project of this size. More concerning was the lack of engagement from senior stakeholders. It felt like we were dealing with mid-level managers who didn't have the authority to make decisions.

Then, there was the broader context. It was 2008 and financial markets were in turmoil.

After discussing it with my team, we made the tough decision to no-bid the opportunity. It wasn't an easy call, walking away from potential revenue never is, but it felt like the right one. And, as it turned out, it was. Just three months later, Lehman Brothers declared bankruptcy and the entire project fell apart.

That experience reaffirmed to me the value of qualifying opportunities out early. By staying disciplined and listening to my instincts, we avoided wasting time, resources and energy on a deal that would have gone nowhere. Sometimes, the best decision you can make in sales is knowing when to say no.

Qualifying the competition

In high-value, complex B2B sales, understanding the competitive landscape is a critical part of qualification. Knowing who your competitors are, their strengths, and their weaknesses enables you to position your solution effectively and pre-empt objections.

Qualifying the competition helps sales teams:

- Anticipate objections: Understand what customers might perceive as advantages of a competitor's solution.
- Differentiate effectively: Highlight unique value propositions that set your offering apart.
- Adjust strategy: Tailor your approach based on the competitive dynamics in the deal.

Five steps to qualify the competition

1. Research thoroughly: Gather information on competitors through customer feedback, industry reports and public data.
2. Ask strategic questions: During the qualification process, subtly inquire about other vendors the customer is considering and their evaluation criteria.
3. Analyse competitive gaps: Identify areas where your solution outshines competitors, such as features, support or pricing - and where you might not match up.
4. Utilise champions: Work with advocates inside the prospect company to understand how competitors are regarded.
5. Plan for head-to-head comparisons: Prepare responses to likely comparisons with competitors, emphasise your value.

By qualifying the competition, salespeople can proactively address challenges, refine their messaging, and enhance their odds of winning the deal.

The competition question

Over the years, I've been in countless customer meetings and watched salespeople ask, *"Who else are you talking to?"* in an effort to unearth which competitors the prospect is engaging. There are a few problems with this question.

- It can feel confrontational or intrusive. Prospects may interpret this question as a defensive tactic rather than a genuine effort to understand their needs.
- It doesn't add immediate value to the conversation. Instead of focusing on the customer's challenges, objectives or decision-making criteria, the question shifts attention to competitors. This can make the salesperson seem more concerned with their competition than with solving the prospect's problems.
- It puts the prospect in an awkward position. Asking directly about competitors might make the prospect feel like they're being put on the spot. They may worry about sharing too much or feel uncertain about how to respond, which could derail the flow of the discussion.
- It's a missed opportunity to demonstrate expertise. Rather than asking about competitors, salespeople can frame the conversation to highlight their unique value and address potential competitive comparisons proactively. This builds confidence in the solution being offered without focusing on others.

The often-overlooked competition: internal challenges

While external competitors often come to mind first, salespeople must also recognise the significant role of competition within the customer organisation. This includes two major hurdles:

- The "do-it-themselves" approach. Many prospects are tempted to solve the problem internally, either by building their own solution, repurposing existing tools or delaying the decision altogether. This approach can seem appealing because it appears to save costs or provide greater control, but it often comes with hidden risks.
- Competition for budgets and resources. Even when a prospect sees the value in your solution, they may face internal struggles to secure approval, budget or resources. Your solution might be competing against other projects or initiatives that align more closely with the company's strategic priorities or immediate needs.

Shifting the Conversation

Rather than asking, "*Who else are you talking to*?" it's more effective to ask questions that explore the prospect's evaluation process and priorities. For example,

- How are you approaching this decision? What factors are most important to you?
- What does your ideal solution look like, and how will you know when you've found it?

- Have you seen any solutions so far that resonate with you, or are there specific challenges you still need to address?

Why all this matters

By addressing both external and internal competition, you demonstrate that you're not just selling a product, you're solving a problem. You show a genuine understanding of the complexities prospects face, from evaluating external options to overcoming internal barriers.

Whether it's helping them articulate the value of your solution to their leadership or guiding them through the risks of a DIY approach, this approach shifts the focus from "the competition" to your prospect's success.

Overcoming common challenges in qualification

Despite its importance, qualification is fraught with challenges. Below are strategies for addressing some of the most common obstacles, which include:

1. Engaging reluctant stakeholders: Not all stakeholders will be eager to engage. Some may view sales interactions as unnecessary or intrusive. To overcome this, emphasise the value of collaboration and tailor your approach to their specific interests and personality types.

2. Managing internal bias: Salespeople often fall victim to confirmation bias, focusing on positive signals while ignoring red flags. Counter this by adopting a disciplined approach to qualification, using frameworks to guide decisions objectively. Also, encourage colleagues to stress test your sales plan and give you objective feedback. Don't fall victim to good news selling as per my example earlier in this chapter.

3. Handling ambiguity: Complex B2B sales are inherently uncertain. Stakeholders may lack clarity on their own needs or processes. In such cases, act as a consultant, helping the customer articulate their priorities and roadmap.

4. Balancing qualification with momentum: Excessive qualification can slow down the sales process, while insufficient qualification can lead to wasted effort. Strive for a balance, ensuring thoroughness without losing momentum. Don't be scared to ask the right questions, but don't turn it into the Spanish inquisition.

By embracing a structured and disciplined approach, sales people can focus their resources where they will have the most impact, leading to a more efficient use of resources and higher success rates.

Exercise: Effective qualification in B2B sales

Objective: To develop a structured and actionable approach for qualifying high-value, complex sales opportunities and deciding when to pursue or disqualify opportunities.

Step 1: Build Your Qualification Plan: Use the following framework to evaluate a sales opportunity.

Understand the customer's challenge:

- What specific problems or challenges are they trying to solve?
- Why are these challenges critical now?
- What is the potential impact of solving these challenges?

Identify stakeholders and decision-makers:

- Who holds the budget?
- Who are the influencers and end users?
- Are there potential detractors and how can you address their concerns?

Evaluate the budget:

- Is there an approved budget?
- If not, what is the process for budget approval?
- Does their budget align with the value of your solution?

Establish the compelling event:

- What is driving the timeline for this initiative?
- What happens if the timeline slips?

Assess fit and feasibility:

- Does your solution align with their needs and constraints?

- Are there technical or operational barriers?

Step 2: Implement key qualification steps: Choose actionable steps to apply to a current or future potential opportunity, as below:

Conduct a qualification call: Use open-ended questions to uncover challenges, budget, and decision-making processes. Ask questions like:

- What challenges are you currently facing that you're looking to address with this initiative?
- What's your typical process for approving budgets and solutions like this?
- Who else in your organisation is involved in evaluating and deciding on this solution?

Map the decision-making unit: Create a list of stakeholders, their roles, and their priorities, for example:

- CFO: Prioritises cost efficiency and ROI.
- IT director: Focuses on technical feasibility.
- End users: Interested in ease of use and functionality.

Qualify the budget and timeline: Ask about urgency and funding, with question like:

- What is your desired implementation date and is there an approved budget to meet that timeline?
- What happens if this project is delayed or doesn't move forward?

Practice

Choose three of the prospects in your pipeline and apply your qualification plan to them. They could be new prospects or ones further down your pipeline you want to requalify.

- Identify key qualification questions you would ask.
- Map the decision-making unit and their likely priorities.
- Decide whether you would qualify this opportunity in or out based on your findings.

Practice makes perfect

After qualifying your opportunities, reflect on the following:

Clarity: Did your questions uncover enough detail to evaluate the opportunity's viability?

Alignment: Did the opportunity align with your solution and resources?

Next Steps: What actions will you take to move forward. Or why have you decided to qualify it out?

Chapter 11: Asking the right questions

In B2B sales, asking the right questions is one of the most effective tools in a salesperson's toolkit. Asking the right questions help you uncover needs, understand challenges, build rapport, establish credibility and demonstrate that you are genuinely interested in solving the customer's problems.

But not all questions are created equal. The questions you ask and the way ask them can make the difference between a productive, promising conversation and a superficial discussion that leads nowhere. In this chapter we'll explore using different types of questions during customer meetings, including open-ended questions, probing questions, operational questions and more.

Why asking the right questions matters

When done well, asking questions during a customer meeting serves several critical purposes.

- Uncovering needs: The more you understand about the customer's challenges, priorities, and objectives, the better you can tailor your solution to meet their needs.
- Driving the conversation: Good questions turn a one-sided sales pitch into a two-way conversation. They encourage customers to talk, giving you valuable insights.
- Demonstrating value: Thoughtful questions show the customer that you've done your homework and are focused on solving their problems, not just selling your product.
- Building trust: By listening carefully and asking relevant follow-up questions, you show the customer that you care about their success and you know what you're talking about.
- Validating your assumptions: Questions help confirm or challenge your understanding of the customer's needs so you can refine your approach.

Key types of questions

Here's a breakdown of the most important types of questions and when to use them during a customer meeting.

1. Open-ended questions

Open-ended questions encourage the customer to share detailed information. These are particularly effective at the beginning of a meeting when you're gathering insights or trying to set the tone for a collaborative conversation. Open ended questions begin with "what, who, when, why and how, (the general rule is that they cannot be answered with a simple "yes" or "no").

Examples of open-ended questions include:

- What are the biggest challenges your business is currently facing?
- How do you see your business evolving over the next 12 to 18 months?
- Why is the project in-flight at this particular time?
- Where are you in your decision-making process?

Why they work: Open-ended questions invite the customer to speak freely, giving you a broader understanding of their situation. They also help uncover pain points that might not have been apparent initially.

2. Probing questions

Once you've identified an area of interest or challenge, probing questions allow you to dive deeper. These questions help you uncover the "why" behind the issue and identify what's really driving the customer's concerns.

Examples of probing questions include:

- What impact is the current situation having on your business?
- Why do you think that process isn't working as efficiently as it could be?
- How is this issue affecting your team's productivity or ability to meet goals?
- Who is most impacted if this challenge remains unresolved?

Why they work: Probing questions uncover the root cause of problems and provide you with specific details that allow you to tailor your solution more effectively.

3. Operational questions

Operational questions focus on understanding the customer's day-to-day processes, workflows, and systems. These are particularly useful when you're trying to identify inefficiencies, uncover opportunities for improvement or validate your understanding of their business.

Examples of operational questions include:

- How do you currently manage [specific process]?
- What tools or systems are you using to address this issue?
- When do you intend to implement the new (product or service)?
- Why is this date important?

Why they work: Operational questions give you a clearer picture of the customer's processes and workflows, helping you identify where your solution can add the most value.

4. Clarifying questions

These ensure that you fully understand the customer's responses. They are particularly helpful when the customer provides a vague or complex answer, and you need more detail.

Examples of clarifying questions include:

- Just to make sure I understand, you're saying that [summarise their statement], is that correct?
- When you mention 'inefficiencies', can you clarify what specific areas you're referring to?
- Could you give me a real example of how this issue affects your team's work?

Why they work: Clarifying questions help prevent misunderstandings, ensure you're on the same page as the customer and that you are actively listening to them.

5. Validating questions

Validating questions confirm that you've accurately understood the customer's challenges and priorities. These questions are critical for gaining agreement before presenting your solution.

Examples of validating questions include:

- So, if I understand correctly, your main priority is reducing costs in this area, does that align with what you're trying to achieve?
- You mentioned earlier that improving efficiency is a big focus. Would you say that's your top priority right now?
- It sounds like this challenge is affecting your team's performance. Is that a fair summary?

Why they work: Validating questions provide confirmation that you're on the right track, ensuring that your solution will address the customer's real priorities and (again) that you are actively listening to them.

Asking questions that lead to action

The ultimate goal of asking questions is to move the sales process forward. Once you've uncovered their challenges, needs and priorities, you can begin framing the conversation around potential solutions.

Transition questions to move toward the solution include:

- Based on what we've discussed, would it be helpful if I shared how we've solved similar challenges for other clients?
- It sounds like addressing this issue is a priority for you. Would you like to hear how we might be able to help?
- Given what you've shared, I think we have a solution that aligns well with your goals. Can I walk you through it?

These questions shift the conversation from exploration to action while ensuring the customer feels heard and understood.

A key point on this is that if you ask a prospect one of the examples I have given above and they say "no" you're probably not talking to someone genuinely interested in what you are selling and might be better moving on.

Common Pitfalls to Avoid

Even with the right questions, there are a few common mistakes to avoid.

- Asking too many closed questions: Questions that can be answered with "yes" or "no" don't invite discussion and can stall the conversation. Use them sparingly.
- Interrogating the customer: A meeting should feel like a conversation, not an interrogation. Balance your questions with active listening and natural follow-ups.
- Jumping to solutions too early: Resist the urge to immediately pitch your solution. Focus on understanding the customer's needs (and wants) fully before proposing anything.

- Ignoring key responses: If the customer shares a pain point or insight, don't gloss over it. Probe deeper to uncover the full context and impact.

Asking the right questions is the key to productive, insight-driven customer meetings. By using a mix of open-ended, probing, operational, clarifying, and validating questions, you can uncover the real challenges your customers face and position your solution as the answer.

The art of questioning isn't about ticking boxes; it's about engaging the customer in a meaningful conversation that builds trust and uncovers opportunities.

Exercise: Asking the right questions in B2B Sales

Objective: To develop and practice a structured approach for asking questions that uncover customer needs, build rapport, and drive productive conversations.

Step 1: Prepare your question framework

Before your next customer interaction, create a framework using the types of questions outlined in the chapter.

Open-ended questions: Identify two or three broad questions to open the discussion.

- What challenges are you currently facing in your [specific area]?
- How do you see your goals evolving over the next year?

Probing questions: Develop two or three deeper questions to explore pain points and root causes.

- What impact is this challenge having on your team's productivity?
- Why do you think this issue has persisted?

Operational questions: Add one or two specific questions to understand their processes.

- How are you currently managing [specific task]?
- What tools are you using, and how effective are they?

Clarifying questions: Prepare one or two follow-ups to ensure clarity.

- When you say [specific issue], can you give an example?

- Am I understanding correctly that [summarize their response]?

Validating questions: Write one or two questions to confirm your understanding.

- It sounds like improving [specific area] is your priority. Is that correct?
- Would you agree that solving this issue would significantly improve your operations?

Step 2: Implement two or three key steps: Use the following steps to apply your framework in a live or practice scenario:

Plan your opening: Start with one or two open-ended questions to establish rapport and set the tone.

Dive deeper: Use probing and operational questions to uncover the details behind their challenges.

Confirm understanding: Wrap up the discussion with clarifying or validating questions to ensure alignment.

Practice: Choose three prospects in your pipeline and use the examples above to develop a tailored question framework.

- Write two or three open-ended questions, two or three probing questions, and one validating question for your chosen scenario.
- Role-play the conversation with a colleague or in a mock session, focusing on active listening and natural follow-ups.

Practice Makes Perfect After implementing or practicing your framework, reflect on the following:

Effectiveness: Did your questions uncover valuable insights or challenges

Engagement: Did the conversation feel collaborative and natural?

Next Steps: What changes will you make to refine your questioning approach?

My favourite question: The split

In this chapter I've attempted to arm you with a question or technique for every occasion. However, there is one more to share with you, it's my favourite and I ask it during every sales campaign I engage in. It's called "the split."

The split questioning technique

What is it?

The split is a two-part questioning method designed to uncover what the other person values most in a particular subject. It moves beyond surface-level preferences and gets to the heart of *why* something matters to them.

The question is "split" into two components:

- **The subject:** Identify a specific area of interest or experience.
- **The value:** Ask what they appreciated or enjoyed most about it.

This draws out personal insights, helping you understand their preferences, decision-making drivers, and what they truly value.

How it works

Identify the subject matter (the what):
Open with a question about a specific topic.

Explore their values (the why):
Follow it immediately by asking what they liked most about it.

Listen actively:
Give them your full attention, without hijacking the conversation.

Gently prompt for more:
Use natural cues like:

- That sounds brilliant—what else did you enjoy about it?
- Interesting—can you tell me a bit more about that part?

Example 1 – holidays

You: "What's the best holiday you've ever been on?"

Them: "Oh, probably our trip to New Zealand."

You: "That sounds amazing, what did you love most about it"?

Them: "We just felt so free. We rented a campervan and went wherever we wanted, and the scenery was unbelievable."

You (prompting): "That sounds incredible, what part of the freedom or the scenery really stuck with you"?

Them: "I think it was waking up by these beautiful lakes, completely alone, just us and nature."

You: "Wow, that sounds special. What was your favourite spot"?

Example 2 – B2B project management services

You: "Which project management services provider have you worked with that really stood out"?

Them: "Actually, we had a fantastic experience with Acme Projects last year".

You: "Interesting, what did you like most about working with them"?

Them: "They just made everything feel under control. Their communication was so clear and we knew exactly where we stood all the time".

You (prompting): "That's great, sounds like peace of mind was a big factor. Was it their updates, or how they handled issues, that made the difference"?

Them: "Both really. They flagged risks early, so we were never caught off guard."

Example 3 – Sales training company

You: "Which is the best sales training company you've worked with?"

Them: "I'd say johnpc ltd."

You: "And what did you like most about working with them?"

Them: "Their approach was so practical, it wasn't just theory. They tailored everything to our real sales challenges, so we could apply it immediately."

You (prompting): "That's interesting, so it was the customisation and the real-world focus that worked well"?

Them: "Exactly, they actually sat in on a few of our calls to give feedback, which was invaluable."

Final Thought – Spotting the Conversation Thief

Now that you understand the split, here's a fun little challenge:
Start noticing how often people commit "conversation theft" around you.
You'll see it everywhere, someone shares a story about their holiday and within seconds, someone else chimes in with *"Oh, we went to Bali last year!"* or *"I've got that car, it's brilliant!"*

We've *all* been guilty of it. So, also watch yourself, see if you can catch those moments when you're tempted to jump in.
Instead, pause, lean in and give the split a go. You'll be amazed at what you learn when you let the other person stay in the spotlight.

Who knows? You might just become everyone's favourite conversationalist.

Chapter 12: Active listening and reading non-verbal clues

In the last chapter, we explored how effective questioning can uncover valuable insights about a customer's challenges, priorities and objectives.

However, asking the right questions is only half the equation. What truly sets a great B2B salesperson apart is the ability to actively listen to the answers and interpret what's being said (and not said) through non-verbal clues.

Communication in sales is as much about listening and observing as it is about speaking. By paying attention to body language, tone and subtle non-verbal signals, you can gain a deeper understanding of your customer's level of interest, concerns or unspoken objections.

In this chapter we'll focus on two core elements of communication - active listening and reading non-verbal clues. These are practical skills that help you connect with your customers and ensure that you are always one step ahead.

The power of active listening

Active listening goes beyond simply hearing what someone is saying. It's about demonstrating that you're engaged. In a B2B sales environment, active listening helps build trust, uncover critical insights, and guide the conversation effectively.

Too many salespeople fall into the trap of thinking about their next response while the customer is still speaking. This not only undermines rapport, it also causes you to miss valuable information. Active listening ensures you're fully present, responding thoughtfully, and demonstrating genuine interest in solving the customer's problem.

Key principles of active listening

1. **Focus completely on the speaker.** Eliminate distractions, put your phone away, maintain eye contact, and avoid interrupting. Focus on understanding their words and tone rather than mentally preparing your next response.

2. **Listen for meaning.** Pay attention to not just what the customer says, but how they say it. Are there particular words or phrases they emphasise? Does their tone suggest

enthusiasm, hesitation frustration? These clues provide insight into what matters most to them.

3. **Demonstrate engagement.** Show that you're actively listening through small verbal acknowledgments like *"I see," "that makes sense,"* or *"tell me more about that."* Use nodding and facial expressions to reinforce your engagement.

4. **Paraphrase and clarify.** To confirm your understanding, paraphrase what the customer has said and ask for confirmation: "So, if I understand correctly, you're saying that streamlining your operations is a top priority right now. Is that right?"

5. **Ask follow-up questions.** Active listening naturally leads to deeper, more valuable questions. Use follow-ups like: "What impact is that challenge having on your team?" or "Can you give me an example of when this issue came up recently?"

Follow-up questions demonstrate curiosity and encourage the customer to share more insights.

The importance of non-verbal communication

Words are only part of the story. Studies suggest that 70–90% of communication is non-verbal, meaning body language, tone of voice and other non-verbal clues are just as important as the spoken word. In B2B sales meetings, observing these signals can help you identify what your customer is truly thinking or feeling, even if they aren't saying it outright.

Non-verbal clues to watch for

Positive signs of engagement

When customers are interested or aligned with what you're saying, their body language will often give it away.

- Leaning forward: A customer who leans forward, sits up straighter or moves closer to the table is showing interest in the topic. This is one of the clearest signs of engagement.
- Nodding or smiling: Subtle nods, smiles, or encouraging facial expressions indicate they're agreeing with or intrigued by your points.
- Eye contact: Steady eye contact usually suggests trust, attentiveness, and connection with your message.

If you notice these positive signals during your presentation or pitch, take the opportunity to reinforce the point they're interested in. For example, you might say: "I can see this is resonating, would you like me to share more details about how this has worked for other clients"?

Signals of disinterest or concern

Conversely, body language can also signal disinterest, scepticism or discomfort:

- Leaning back or crossed arms: If someone leans back, crosses their arms, or angles their body away from you, it may indicate resistance or disengagement.
- Lack of eye contact: Avoiding eye contact or glancing at their watch or phone often suggests boredom or distraction.
- Frowning or furrowed brows: These subtle expressions may signal confusion, doubt or concern about what you're saying.

If you notice these signals, don't ignore them. Pause and ask a question to re-engage such as, "I sense I might not have explained that clearly, would you like me to elaborate or clarify further?"

Questions as a sign of interest

Remember this simple truth: people only ask questions about things they're interested in. If a customer starts asking you detailed or clarifying questions, this is a strong indicator that they're engaged and considering your solution.

Questions are an opportunity to dive deeper and strengthen the conversation. You might seize upon it by replying, "That's a great question, can I ask what's prompting your interest in that area?"

Use their questions as a chance to reinforce the value of your solution and keep the dialogue flowing.

Combining active listening and non-verbal awareness

The real power comes from combining active listening with a keen awareness of non-verbal signals. When you master both, you're able to:

1. **Pick up on hidden signals**: A prospect might say "I'm not sure about that," while leaning forward and maintaining eye contact. This indicates interest despite their words. Alternatively, they may say "Sounds good," while leaning back with crossed arms, signalling doubt.
2. **Adjust your approach in real time**: By observing body language and listening closely, you can adapt your approach mid-meeting. If a customer seems disengaged, ask a question to bring them back into the conversation. If they show excitement, focus on the points that are resonating most.
3. **Build stronger connections**: Listening carefully and responding to non-verbal signals makes customers feel heard, valued and understood. This builds trust and positions you as someone who truly cares about their challenges.

An opportunity won and an opportunity lost.

Success at Pace Micro

As sales director at Pace Micro, I had the opportunity to pitch for a multi-million-pound contract to supply equipment to a multinational computer manufacturer. The stakes were high, and I knew this was a make-or-break meeting.

From the outset, I focused on active listening and reading the room. During our first meeting, the retailer's purchasing director shared concerns about supply chain reliability. As he spoke, I noticed him leaning forward and maintaining steady eye contact.

His tone conveyed genuine concern, but there was also a hint of curiosity when I mentioned our logistics capabilities. I paused and said, "It sounds like supply chain reliability is a critical factor for you. Would it be helpful if I shared how we've consistently met delivery timelines for clients with similar needs?"

His nod and smile confirmed I was on the right track.

In subsequent meetings, I paid close attention to the reactions of the other stakeholders. The operations manager nodded frequently when I described the technical features of our equipment, but the marketing director seemed disengaged, leaning back with crossed arms. Recognising this, I pivoted and asked, "I sense this might not address all your concerns. What are you thinking about from a customer experience perspective?"

This question unlocked a crucial insight: the marketing director was worried about after-sales service and customer satisfaction. By addressing this head-on and presenting robust support options, I turned a potential roadblock into a point of trust.

Ultimately, by listening actively and adjusting to both verbal and non-verbal signals, I won their confidence. They awarded us the contract, and the relationship became one of our most successful partnerships.

Missed opportunity at Case Communications

When I was sales director at Case Communications in New Zealand, we had the chance to bid for a lucrative communications network upgrade for an airliner. I went into the meetings confident, but in hindsight, I was too focused on presenting our technical capabilities and not enough on truly listening to their concerns.

During the initial pitch, the airliner's project lead mentioned their need for a seamless transition with minimal disruption to operations. Instead of probing further, I launched into a technical presentation about our product's features. While I was talking, I noticed the COO shift in his seat, glance at his watch, and eventually lean back with his arms crossed. Rather than addressing these non-verbal signals, I pressed on, eager to finish my points.

When questions arose, I missed the deeper meaning behind them. For example, the CFO asked, "How does your solution compare to competitors on cost predictability?" I gave a general response about competitive pricing but failed to ask why this was a priority. I later learned their previous supplier had caused budget overruns, a pain point I could have addressed had I listened and probed further.

In the final meeting, I noticed several key stakeholders seemed disengaged, their body language closed off and their questions minimal. Instead of adjusting my approach, I stuck to my script, assuming my technical presentation would win them over.

We lost the contract to a competitor who, I later learned, had tailored their proposal to address the company's operational and financial concerns. My failure to actively listen and respond to both verbal and non-verbal cues had cost us a significant opportunity.

Actionable steps to improvement

Here are some actionable steps to improve your ability to ask the right questions, listen actively, and observe non-verbal clues.

Before the meeting:

- Prepare three or four open-ended questions to uncover your customer's priorities.
- Revisit any prior conversations for clues about concerns or areas of interest.

During the meeting

- Use active listening techniques, focus fully, paraphrase, and ask follow-up questions.

Watch for non-verbal clues:

- Leaning forward = interest.
- Crossed arms or lack of eye contact = disengagement or concern.

Pause and clarify when needed

- I get the sense this might not align perfectly with what you're looking for. Is there something I've missed?

After the meeting:

- Reflect on the customer's verbal and non-verbal responses. Did you notice patterns? Which areas generated interest, and which raised concerns? Use this to guide your follow-up.

Effective communication in B2B sales is not just about speaking clearly, it's about listening intently and interpreting what the customer is truly saying, both verbally and non-verbally. By mastering active listening and observing body language, you'll gain deeper insights, strengthen trust and keep the conversation focused on what matters most to the customer.

Exercise: Active listening and reading non-verbal clues

Objective: To enhance your ability to actively listen and interpret non-verbal clues during meetings with existing prospects or customers, enabling deeper engagement and more productive conversations.

Step 1: Preparation

Review previous interactions:

Revisit notes or correspondence to identify key topics of interest, concerns, or unspoken signals from past meetings.

Develop a question framework

Prepare two or three open-ended questions designed to uncover insights. Examples include:

- What are the key priorities for your team this quarter?
- How has the current situation impacted your goals?

Set an observation goal:

- Identify one specific non-verbal signal you'll pay closer attention to, such as body language, tone shifts, or eye contact.

Step 2: Implement during the meeting

Practice active listening

- Eliminate distractions (phone or laptop notifications).
- Paraphrase key points to confirm understanding: "So, you're saying that improving efficiency in this area is critical right now. Is that correct?"
- Ask follow-up questions to dive deeper: "Can you share an example of when this challenge impacted your team recently?"

Observe non-verbal clues

- Look for positive signals (leaning forward, nodding, steady eye contact).
- Note disengagement cues (crossed arms, lack of eye contact, fidgeting).

Respond in real time

- If you notice positive engagement, reinforce the topic: "I can see this resonates. Would you like me to elaborate further on this point?"
- If you observe disengagement, address it gently: "I sense this might not be exactly what you were expecting. Can you share more about what's on your mind?"

Step 3: Reflect after the meeting

Analyse engagement:

- What verbal and non-verbal signals stood out?
- Which topics generated the most interest, and which raised concerns?

Evaluate your listening skills:

- Did you paraphrase effectively to confirm understanding?
- Were your follow-up questions insightful and aligned with the customer's concerns?

Plan next steps:

- How will you use the insights gained to tailor your follow-up?
- If disengagement occurred, how can you address it in your next interaction?

Practice: Choose one of your most important prospects and ask a colleague(s) to role play your meeting plan, with one or more of them acting as the customer.

- Practice observing verbal and non-verbal cues in the chosen scenario.
- Draft one follow-up question and one clarification question to address potential concerns or disengagement.

Practice makes perfect

- How did active listening and non-verbal observations impact the conversation?
- Did you identify hidden concerns or unspoken objections?
- What will you improve for future meetings to strengthen trust and engagement?

Chapter 13: Understanding customer personality types

In B2B sales, success often comes down to how well you can connect with your customers. While understanding their business challenges and priorities is vital, understanding how they think, behave, and make decisions can elevate your ability to build rapport and earn trust.

Over the years, a range of tools and frameworks has been developed to help us identify and work with different personality types. Popular examples include Myers-Briggs Type Indicator (MBTI), which classifies people into 16 distinct personality types; Insights Discovery, which uses a colour-based model to describe behaviour and Belbin Team Roles, which focuses on individuals' strengths in team settings.

Each of these tools has its merits, and all can provide valuable insights into how people prefer to work and communicate. However, my personal preference, based on its simplicity, practicality, and effectiveness in a sales environment is Wiley's Everything DiSC.

DiSC stands for,

- Dominance.
- Influence.
- Steadiness.
- Conscientiousness.

Everything DiSC categorises individuals based on these four behavioural traits. This is the system I've used in my johnpc ltd sales training workshops over the last 15 years. Using Everything DiSC has enabled me to learn a tremendous amount about human nature and about myself.

In this chapter, I'll break down the DiSC personality types, explain their key characteristics and share practical tips on how to engage and communicate effectively with each type in a B2B sales context.

Why understanding personality types matters

When you approach a customer meeting, you're not just dealing with a job title or a business decision-maker, you're engaging with a person. Like all of us, their personality will influence how they communicate, process information, make decisions, and respond to your solution. By understanding personality types, you can:

- Adjust your communication style to suit their preferences.
- Anticipate their likely concerns, behaviours, and priorities.
- Tailor your approach to build trust and rapport faster.

In short, knowing how to "speak their language" makes you more effective and helps move the sales conversation forward. As you read through the next section think about your current customers and see how you think they fall into any of the DiSC personality types.

The four DiSC personality types

The Everything DiSC model categorises people into four primary personality types: Dominance (D), Influence (i), Steadiness (S), and Conscientiousness (C). It's important to note that nobody is purely one type; most people are a blend of all four, with one or two traits being more dominant. Let's explore each type and how you can adapt your approach accordingly. It's also important to stress that no particular type is better suited to any particular type of role.

Dominance (D): The results and control focus

People with a high "D" personality are direct, decisive, and results-oriented. They value efficiency, control, and bottom-line results. They tend to be assertive and competitive. In meetings, they prefer to get straight to the point and can become impatient with unnecessary (and sometimes necessary) detail or small talk.

How to spot them

- They speak confidently and directly and seek to gain control.
- They are often the first to ask about timelines or outcomes.
- They may interrupt or push for quick decisions.

Tips for dealing with dominant types

- Be direct and concise: Avoid long-winded explanations; get to the point quickly.
- Focus on results: Emphasise measurable outcomes, benefits, and efficiency. For example, "this solution will reduce your operational costs by 20% within six months."
- Show confidence: Be assertive and speak with authority, don't waffle or appear unsure.
- Be prepared for challenges: Expect tough questions and a desire to cut through ambiguity. Be ready with clear, factual answers.

Influence (i): The social and enthusiastic collaborator

People with "i" personalities are outgoing, enthusiastic and people-oriented. They thrive on interaction, enjoy collaboration and are often natural networkers. These individuals are driven by relationships and are motivated by recognition, excitement, and new ideas. They can, however, be less focused on details, processes and achieving specific tangible outcomes.

How to spot them

- They're energetic, expressive and talkative.
- They enjoy sharing stories and ideas and may lean toward optimism.
- They're quick to show enthusiasm for new concepts or opportunities.

Tips for dealing with influencing types

- Build rapport early: Spend time engaging in friendly, natural conversation to connect with them on a personal level.
- Be enthusiastic and engaging: Match their energy and excitement. Present your solution in a way that inspires and energises them.
- Focus on the "big picture": Highlight how your solution helps them achieve their objectives and stand out. Avoid getting bogged down in technical details too soon.
- Use stories and examples: They respond well to anecdotes, case studies, and examples of success.

Example: "One of our customers, a fast-growing tech firm, faced similar challenges. After implementing this solution, their team saw a 30% boost in productivity."

Steadiness (S): The reliable and supportive partner

People with "S" personalities are calm, dependable and team-oriented. They value stability, consistency and relationships built on trust. They are often patient listeners, thoughtful decision-makers and prefer to avoid conflict. They appreciate being supported and reassured throughout the decision-making process.

How to spot them

- They are warm, approachable, and thoughtful in their responses.
- They may take time to consider information and are hesitant to rush decisions.

- They show loyalty to vendors they trust and relationships they value.

Tips for dealing with steady types

- Build trust over time: Focus on creating a safe and comfortable space for discussion. Demonstrate patience and reliability.
- Offer reassurance; address concerns proactively and provide clarity around risks, next steps, or timelines.
- Avoid high-pressure tactics; they dislike being rushed. Give them time to process information and consult with others.
- Focus on support and long-term benefit; highlight how your solution will make their work easier and contribute to consistent success over time.

Example: "We'll provide full onboarding support to ensure a smooth transition and our team will be on hand throughout to assist if any issues arise."

Conscientiousness (C): The detail-oriented analyst

High "C" personalities are precise, analytical and results-oriented. They value accuracy, quality, and well-thought-out solutions. These individuals are often cautious decision-makers who want to weigh all the facts before committing to a course of action. They may ask probing questions to ensure your solution meets their standards. (Note this is my personality type).

How to spot them

- They ask detailed, technical questions
- They're methodical in their approach and may focus on risks, data, or processes
- They are less likely to make emotional decisions and more likely to rely on logic and evidence.

Tips for dealing with conscientious types

- Be prepared with data: Back up your claims with facts, metrics and case studies. They respond well to logic and evidence.
- Provide detail: Share specifics about your solution, processes, and timelines. Be ready for follow-up questions.

- Avoid ambiguity: Be clear, organised and thorough in your explanations. For example: "Here's a detailed breakdown of the implementation process, including milestones and responsibilities."
- Give them time: Conscientious types may need time to analyse information. Be patient and follow up with additional resources if needed.

Bringing it all together

Understanding customer personality types using the DiSC model allows you to adapt your approach and communicate in a way that resonates with your audience; the key is to recognise their preferences and adjust your tone, pace and content accordingly.

Practical tips for applying DiSC in customer meetings

1. **Observe and adapt**: Pay attention to verbal and non-verbal cues during the meeting. How are they communicating? What do they emphasise?
2. **Stay flexible**: Remember that people are rarely purely one type. Be prepared to adjust your approach as the conversation evolves
3. **Focus on their priorities**: Tailor your communication to what matters most to their personality type; results, relationships, stability, or accuracy
4. **Build stronger connections**: By understanding and respecting their preferences, you can build trust faster and move toward a positive outcome.

Understanding customer personality types isn't about putting people into boxes, it's about recognising and respecting their differences. Tools like Wiley's Everything DiSC provide a simple yet effective framework for identifying key behaviours and adapting your approach to suit your customer.

By engaging with customers in a way that aligns with their personality type, you create stronger relationships, uncover deeper insights, and ultimately position yourself as someone they want to buy from.

Invest in yourself

If you genuinely interested in gaining a better understanding of yourself and improving your ability to communicate with others, I'd strongly recommend you invest in doing an Everything DiSC online assessment and maybe even attending a one-day training course to develop and hone your skills.

From DISC to Diana: The multifaceted mind of William Marston

Once upon a time, in the dynamic world of the early 20th century, a man named William Moulton Marston wore more hats than a milliner's shop could stock. Psychologist, inventor, writer and feminist, Marston didn't just think outside the box, he invented the box. Several boxes.

Among his many accomplishments, he created the DiSC personality assessment and Wonder Woman, two contributions that, on the surface, seem to have little in common. But perhaps they're more connected than we realise.

It all started with Marston's fascination with human behaviour. A pioneer in psychology, he wanted to decode what made people tick. His work led to the DiSC theory, a framework for understanding relationships, leadership styles, and teamwork. Who wouldn't want a tool to navigate the chaos of human interactions?

But Marston's creative mind didn't stop there. While he was untangling the threads of personality, he also found inspiration in his belief in female empowerment. Marston envisioned a character who embodied his ideals of justice, love, and equality, Wonder Woman. Armed with a Lasso of Truth (a playful nod to his invention of the lie detector), Diana Prince burst onto the comic book scene, smashing patriarchy and villains in equal measure.

Wonder Woman could be seen as a living embodiment of the DiSC traits: her Dominance in battle, her Influence as a symbol of hope, her Steadiness in her values and her Conscientiousness in her mission for justice. Was Wonder Woman secretly a DiSC assessment brought to life? Perhaps Marston, with his knack for blending science and storytelling, intended it that way.

Imagine if Wonder Woman handed you a DiSC profile instead of her lasso:
"Your Dominance is strong but maybe dial back the 'Amazons are always right' attitude! Oh, and your Conscientiousness? It could use some work - you left your sword in the invisible jet again."

Marston's legacy is a testament to his belief in understanding and empowering others. Whether you're using the DiSC assessment to navigate a team meeting or channelling your inner Wonder Woman to conquer the day, you're living proof of his vision; that the mind and heart, when aligned, can change the world.

So if and when you take a DiSC assessment, remember the man behind the theory and the woman behind the man. Somewhere out there, Marston is smiling, knowing his creations continue to inspire us to understand ourselves and better understand others; preferably while wearing bulletproof bracelets.

Chapter 14: Writing winning sales proposals

"Don't tell me how good you make it; tell me how good it makes me when I use it." – Leo Burnett.

Why sales proposals fail

Imagine walking into a tailor's shop for a bespoke suit. You expect measurements to be taken, fabrics discussed and a design tailored specifically to your needs. Instead, the tailor disappears into the back room, grabs a premade suit off the rack and hands it to you without any adjustments. Would you feel valued or confident that the suit fits perfectly?

This is what happens when a salesperson builds a proposal by cutting and pasting boilerplate content from an old template. It lacks customisation, fails to reflect the customer's unique needs and ultimately leaves the client feeling like just another transaction.

Unfortunately, this is what is happening in sales offices up and down the country right now.

Crafting a proposal is like tailoring a suit. It should fit the customer perfectly, addressing their challenges, objectives and priorities. A well-crafted, personalised proposal demonstrates professionalism and commitment, leaving a lasting impression and significantly improving your chances of success.

In this chapter I'll focus on mastering the art and science of proposal writing, a vital yet often overlooked sales skill. Many salespeople lack formal training, relying instead on trial-and-error methods, which more often than not result in rushed, inconsistent, and unpersuasive efforts.

What is a proposal?

A proposal is more than just a sales document, it's your "silent salesperson". Once you leave the customer's office, your proposal is the sole representation of your ideas and the benefits your solution brings. This alone underscores the importance of delivering a proposal that is clear, compelling and impactful.

A proposal should be:

- A collaborative effort involving you, your team (if you're part of one) and the customer.
- A clear demonstration of your understanding and capability.

- The solution you are recommending to help the customer achieve their objectives.
- Concise, easy to read, and to the point.

A proposal should not be:

- A technical document created in isolation.
- A boiler plate, cut and paste rehash of a previous proposal.
- A document that lacks the detail necessary to justify moving forward.
- Difficult to read, complex and confusing.

A well-crafted proposal speaks for you in your absence and creates a lasting impression.

The challenges of writing successful proposals

Creating successful proposals involves overcoming two key challenges, one for readers and one for writers.

1. Challenges customers face when reading proposals: Customers often struggle with:

- Extracting key points from dense text.
- Comparing multiple proposals from different companies.
- Limited time to read and evaluate.
- Maintaining interest throughout a lengthy proposal.
- Understanding complex technical information.
- Trusting the validity of claims made.
- Comparing proposals fairly and comprehensively.
- Grasping the full scope of the solution being proposed.

By getting these points correct, you will make the reading experience smoother and leave a positive impression.

2. Challenges writers face when developing proposals: Proposal writers frequently:

- Struggle to articulate accurately the client's needs.
- Lack insight into the audience or the proposal's true purpose.
- Fail to address diverse readers with varying expertise.
- Struggle to collaborate effectively with a team.
- Find it hard to maintain consistency in tone, style and structure.
- Lack the skills or tools for efficient proposal writing.

Characteristics of successful proposals

A successful proposal enables the client to make a favourable decision. It distinguishes you from competitors, advances the sales process and effectively communicates your ideas and offerings.

Key characteristics of successful proposals

- Have something to say: Present a clear, compelling message.
- Capture attention: Engage the reader from the start and maintain their interest.
- Reinforce key points: Repeat important messages throughout for emphasis.
- Avoid boilerplate content: Customise the proposal to the client's unique situation.
- Make it readable: Ensure content is easy to read and understand.
- Be complete: Leave no essential questions unanswered.

By addressing these characteristics, you'll create proposals that not only meet client needs but also position you as a trusted and professional partner.

Proposal structure

While proposals may vary, they need a clear structure to align with customer expectations. Just like any good story, a proposal should have a beginning, middle and end. Consisting of an introduction, a main body and a conclusion. Deviating too far from this familiar structure can confuse the reader and dilute your message.

The SOMQCB framework

The following six-step structure, known as SOMQCB, is a proven and effective model for developing successful proposals. Not only does it improve proposal writing, but it also deepens your understanding of customer needs, opportunities, solutions and your own capabilities.

SOMQCB Sections

1. Situation: Outline your understanding of the customer's problem or opportunity.
2. Objectives: State the objectives for solving the problem or realizing the opportunity.
3. Methods: Describe your solution and the methods you will use to achieve the objectives.
4. Qualifications: Highlight your qualifications and expertise to implement the methods.
5. Costs: Present the costs associated with your solution and methods.

6. Benefits: Demonstrate the value and benefits the customer will gain from your solution.

Can I always use SOMQCB?

It depends. If the customer dictates the structure of your proposal, SOMQCB may not be practical. However, you can often use it to structure the Executive Summary.

By using SOMQCB and organising your proposal effectively, you can ensure clarity, coherence, and a stronger impact on your customer.

The situation section

The situation section is vital, especially in competitive scenarios with similar offerings and costs. Often titled, "Background" or "Our understanding of your situation", this section introduces your proposal and demonstrates your knowledge of the customers, industry, organisation, and challenges.

Key elements include:

- Who: Show you understand who the customer is and what they do.
- Background: Describe how this opportunity arose and key players involved.
- Causes: Identify factors leading to the problem or opportunity.
- Problem/opportunity: Clearly define the issue or opportunity.
- Effects: Highlight consequences of inaction or unrealised opportunities.
- Attempted solutions: Detail previous efforts and outcomes.

A well-crafted situation section ensures the customer feels understood, encouraging deeper engagement with your proposal. Thorough research is essential to address vague or incomplete customer input and build a strong business case.

Remember what we covered in the chapter on qualification; good qualification is key to getting the situation (and the objectives) sections correct.

The objectives section

The objectives section outlines the customer's aims, what they hope to achieve by spending their organisation's money and proceeding with your proposal. This section defines the "To Be" scenario, setting the stage for your methods section by contrasting it with the "As Is" current situation.

Key considerations for objectives

- What does the customer want to accomplish?
- What are their priorities? Present the objectives clearly and rank them in importance.
- Why are these priorities important? Add context and highlight the value of achieving each objective.
- Be concise: Only include objectives you can address in the proposal.

Remember, a single well-defined objective is often more effective than a long list of vague ones. Incorporate the customer's language and terminology to reflect their perspective and priorities.

The methods section

The methods slot explains *how* you will take the customer from their current *"As Is"* situation to their desired *"To Be"* state. It should address three key elements,

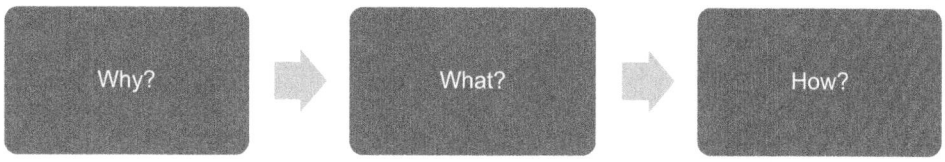

- Why? Justify your chosen approach. Explain why this solution is the best among possible options, and share insights into the process of selecting this method.
- What? Define the solution or offering. Present the solution clearly using diagrams, tables, or text as appropriate. Tailor the level of detail to the audience's needs.
- How? Outline the actions required to implement the solution. Detail what will happen, why it's necessary and how it will be executed. Include project plans, timelines and milestones to give clarity on execution.

The methods section not only explains your approach but also reassures the customer of its feasibility and effectiveness, building confidence in your ability to deliver.

The qualifications section

The qualifications section focuses on demonstrating why your solution is the best choice for the project by aligning your abilities and capabilities with the customer's needs.

- **Abilities**: Highlight qualities of your team, such as experience, expertise, and personal characteristics.
- **Capabilities**: Showcase company resources, proprietary methodologies or models that strengthen your case.

This section should centre around the claim, "We are the best qualified company for this project because…" Every detail provided should directly support this claim.

Key points for the qualifications section

- Include evidence of significant experience implementing similar solutions.
- Provide examples of prior successes, customer references and recommendations.
- Avoid generic "boilerplate" content.
- Keep the section concise with additional details placed in an appendix if necessary.

A well-crafted qualifications section should leave the customer confident that your solution is perfectly suited for their project.

The Cost section

While cost is a crucial element, it's often not the sole factor in a customer's decision. Customers care just as much about the value they'll receive as they do about the price. A strong proposal addresses both.

Guidelines for presenting costs,

- Present costs clearly and concisely, using tables where appropriate.
- Qualify budgets and customer expectations early.
- Highlight any variables or estimates to manage expectations.

Remember, cost alone won't win the deal. It must be framed within the broader context of the value and benefits your solution provides.

The benefits section

The benefits section is your opportunity to answer the critical customer question, "Why should I buy from you?" It describes the specific value your product or service will deliver.

Crafting an effective benefits section

- Directly relate the benefits to the project's objectives. Avoid including superfluous benefits that don't align with the client's stated goals. People aren't interested in what your solution does. They're interested in what it does for them.
- Use the "base logic" framework: You are here (As Is), you want to be there (To Be) and when you get there, these are the benefits you will gain.
- If additional advantages exist outside the stated objectives, present them as "additional benefits" rather than core benefits.

Benefits often include:

- Increased sales.
- Improved operational efficiency.
- Time and cost savings.
- Competitive advantage.

A strong benefits section solidifies the value of your solution, ensuring the customer understands how your proposal meets their needs and creates tangible results.

Three-phase proposal writing process

Writing a winning proposal involves three key phases,

> **Pre-writing.** This is the most critical phase, focused on preparation, planning, and analysis before drafting begins. Key tasks include:

- Analysing the audience.
- Establishing the proposal's base logic.
- Defining your approach.
- Outlining content using a structured worksheet.

> **Writing the Draft.** During this phase, information is analysed, organised and presented for maximum readability and relevance to the audience.

- The primary task here is producing an outline draft of your proposal. We will cover this in greater detail in the "Developing Your Skills" section at the end of this chapter.

Editing and polishing. The final phase ensures the proposal is persuasive and error-free, ready for reading and presentation. Tasks include editing for:

- Clarity and impact.
- Persuasiveness.
- Grammar and accuracy.

By following this structured process, you can create polished, professional proposals tailored to your customer's needs.

Analysing the audience

Understanding your audience is essential for creating a successful proposal. By identifying your readers and addressing their pain points, problems and objectives, you can build immediate support for your proposal.

Types of audiences

Proposals typically involve a mix of internal, external, visible and hidden audiences,

- External audience: Individuals in the customer's organisation who formally read and evaluate the proposal.
- Internal audience: Members of your own organisation who may review or contribute to the proposal.
- Visible audience: Known individuals in both organisations who will officially receive and read the proposal.
- Hidden audience: Informal readers who may influence the decision-making process.

Identifying key players

Key players are decision-makers, recommenders or influencers within the customer's organisation. Analysing them in detail helps tailor your proposal to their needs and concerns. Consider:

- Names, titles and roles in the decision-making process.
- Their stance on your company and solution.
- Their level of knowledge about their needs and the proposal subject.
- Specific focuses, personality types, and drivers.
- How they perceive change and what they expect from your proposal.

Results of audience analysis

Effective audience analysis enables you to create targeted proposals that:

- Address specific needs and concerns.
- Answer questions, alleviate fears and reduce opposition.
- Build a connection with each audience member.

Properly aimed proposals not only inform but also inspire a desire for your product or service, improving the likelihood of success.

Proposal strategy and approach

Developing a clear proposal strategy during the pre-writing phase is crucial. It helps you plan the organisation and content of the proposal, emphasising key points while minimising less relevant details.

Key focus areas

- **Base logic**
  The foundation of your proposal:
  "You are here (As Is), and you want to be there (To Be). When you get to there (To Be), these are the benefits you will receive."
  A solid base logic ensures your proposal addresses the customer's current situation and desired outcomes. Without it, the proposal risks becoming a simple pricing document.
- **Competitor analysis**
  Assess your strengths and weaknesses compared to competitors. Use this insight to emphasise your advantages and capitalise on competitor weaknesses.
- **Audience-specific content customisation**
  Tailor content for each audience segment. For example, provide detailed cost breakdowns for financially focused readers or highlight technical features for innovation-driven stakeholders.
- **Resonating focus**
  Identify and address topics that resonate with decision-makers, such as aligning with their specific objectives or values.

- **Proposal description**

    Outline the key attributes of your proposal. What are its main themes and strengths? How will it look? How would you describe it to others?

By addressing these areas, you can craft a compelling, targeted proposal that resonates with your audience.

The base logic process

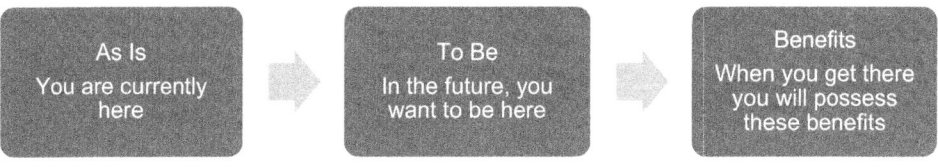

Proposal title

A point to stress here, is that the title of your proposal should capture the benefit its implementation will bring to the customer. For example, if I'm hired to deliver a sales skills workshop on negotiation to a sales team, with the objective being to increase the customer's profit margins, the proposal won't carry the title "negotiation course", it will be called "increasing profits at XYZ company."

This strategy shows the customer you know what they want to achieve and that's what the outcome is focused on.

Developing your proposal outline

Creating your proposal outline is the next step after defining your proposal strategy. This outline provides a high-level framework for each section of the proposal and serves as a roadmap for writing the first draft.

Begin by considering the standard components of a proposal. For each section, brainstorm the key points and ideas to include, guided by your audience analysis and strategic approach.

Once the content outline is ready, you can:

- Delegate specific sections to members of your proposal writing team.

- Share the outline with the team to gather feedback and refine your approach.

The outline ensures a cohesive, well-organised proposal and streamlines the writing process, whether handled by a team or just by you.

Your proposal should use clear, concise and direct language, avoiding unnecessary complexity, clichés, or overly sophisticated phrasing. Simplicity and clarity ensure effective communication. Make it as easy to read as possible. Write as you would speak.

The situation and objectives section should be written first. Ask yourself, do you have a clear understanding of where the customer currently is and where they want to get to?

The method, qualifications, costs and benefits should be written next. Ask yourself, does your offer satisfy the customer's requirements (organisational and personal) and align with their timescales and budgets?

Executive summary

You may be wondering why I've left it so late in the chapter to talk about the executive summary? The simple reason is that it's the last thing you write. You can't "summarise" your proposal until it's complete.

An executive summary highlights the key points of a proposal and convinces your customer of its value in just a few paragraphs. Since many customers may only review this section, it should:

- Clearly demonstrate your understanding of the customer's situation and what they want to achieve.
- Clearly state what you propose to do and how you propose to do it.
- Highlight the benefits the customer can expect.

Make the entire focus of your executive summary the customer, their challenges and the benefits you bring. Ensure it's about them, not about you.

Remember it's a summary. No matter how large or complicated your proposal, the summary should be limited to one, maximum two, pages

Personally, I always put the cost headline number in the executive summary, because:

- You should always discuss how much you want for your solution before you send your proposal (unless it's a closed tender scenario and the rules prevent you from doing so).
- If you truly believe your offer is value for money, there's no need to hide your price on page 37. Lead with it: if you've done a good qualification job, the benefits will justify the price.

Pulling it all together

Writing a winning proposal requires a structured approach to ensure clarity, persuasiveness and alignment with customer needs. In this chapter I've outlined key components for successful proposals, starting with the SOMQCB framework, which organises proposals into logical sections.

Understanding your audience and crafting content tailored to their needs is critical, as is addressing both their challenges and the benefits of buying from you. Clear, concise language, combined with a strong base logic, reinforces your message and ensures your proposal is easy to read and impactful.

Hopefully, I've emphasised the importance of developing a clear strategy, creating a detailed content outline and editing for clarity and coherence. Finally, the executive summary, written last, should focus on the customer, summarising key points, benefits and costs. By applying these principles, you can create winning proposals that stand out and drive results.

Exercise: Creating an outline draft proposal

To apply the concepts from this chapter, complete the following exercise based on a current sales opportunity in your pipeline.

1. **Identify the opportunity**
   - Select a sales opportunity where a proposal will be needed.

2. **Define the situation and objectives**
   - Outline the customer's current situation (As Is) and where they want to be (To Be)
   - Clearly state the objectives the customer wants to achieve.

3. **Draft the SOMQCB framework**
   - Using the SOMQCB framework, create a basic outline for your proposal.

4. **Personalise key sections**
   - Identify at least one specific way to customise the proposal for your customer (tailoring language, focusing on a point of resonating focus or presenting unique benefits).

5. **Review and edit**
   - Edit for clarity, persuasiveness, and impact.
   - Ensure the language is concise and focused on the customer's needs.

6. **Share with colleagues for feedback and critique**

7. **Compare and contrast with your previous proposals.**

Chapter 15: Presenting your proposal

"There are always three speeches for every one you actually gave, the one you practiced, the one you gave and the one you wish you'd given" – Dale Carnegie.

A well-written proposal is a powerful tool and its impact is maximised when you deliver it personally. Presenting your proposal in person, whether that's face-to-face or virtually in a formal or informal setting, gives you the opportunity to connect, clarify and emphasise your value.

While some salespeople might default to sending their proposal via email, this approach misses a critical moment; the opportunity to control the narrative, gauge the customer's reactions and engage directly with questions or concerns.

Delivering your proposal isn't about being a brilliant presenter; it's about creating a professional, confident and engaging experience that moves the opportunity forward. Even in informal settings, the ability to present forms part of any successful salesperson's skill set.

I was once invited to an informal meeting with the IT director of local council in central England. On arrival I was somewhat surprised that (even though I had been told it was a one-to-one meeting), their plans had changed and I was asked to present to the council members (circa 20 people) in the council chambers. With no preparation and no visual aids, I talked them through it using a flipchart. Fortunately, I was relatively well prepared and did enough to win the deal. Always prepare because you never know.

In this chapter I'll focus on a tried-and-tested presentation technique, the Open-Body-Conclusion format, whilst also highlighting practical tips like making an emotional connection, practicing your delivery and setting a clear call to action.

The discussion document tactic

Before we delve into the detail, I want to share a tactic with you called, "the discussion document" that has worked for me on countless occasions.

A powerful tactic for engaging your customer and refining your proposal is to present it as a "discussion document". The premise is simple: instead of presenting a fully polished proposal upfront, you frame it as a draft designed for collaborative discussion and feedback.

How it works:

1. **Prepare your draft proposal**
   Create a draft version of your proposal (see chapter 14).
2. **Position it as a discussion document**
   Contact the customer and explain that you've prepared a discussion document you'd like to walk through with them. Emphasise that their input is valuable and will help tailor the final proposal to meet their exact requirements.
3. **Engage in a collaborative review**
   Arrange a meeting to review the document together, actively listening to their feedback, clarifying their concerns and noting any adjustments needed.
4. **Refine and submit**
   Incorporate the customer's insights and finalise the proposal, ensuring it reflects their preferences and priorities. This way, the final document is transformed from a proposal to a collaborative solution.

Benefits of the discussion document approach:

- **Builds customer engagement**: Inviting feedback makes the customer feel involved and valued, creating a sense of partnership.
- **Ensures alignment**: The collaborative process ensures your final proposal aligns closely with the customer's expectations.
- **Identifies objections early**: By discussing the draft, you uncover and address potential objections before submitting the final proposal.
- **Increases win rates**: A proposal refined with customer input is more likely to resonate and result in a favourable decision.

By positioning your draft as a discussion document, you shift the dynamic from a one-sided presentation to a collaborative problem-solving exercise; significantly increasing your chances of success.

Why you should personally present your proposal

Presenting your proposal is not just about reading aloud what's in a document. It's about bringing your solution to life and ensuring your audience understands the value you bring. Here's why presenting your proposal matters:

- **You control the message.**
  You have the chance to explain the proposal in your own words, emphasise key points and ensure nothing is misunderstood.

- **You make an emotional connection.**
  Your tone, energy and enthusiasm build rapport and show the customer that you care about their challenges and objectives
- **You can handle questions and objections in real time.**
  By presenting in person, you can address concerns immediately, preventing doubts from lingering concerns
- **You demonstrate confidence and professionalism.**
  A strong, clear presentation reassures the customer that they are dealing with someone credible and capable.

While there will be times when presenting in person isn't possible, perhaps due to scheduling, geography, or preference, you should aim for a live presentation wherever possible. If you're presenting virtually, the same rules apply. Treat it as a formal event, even if the audience is remote.

Structuring your presentation: Open, body, conclusion

The Open-Body-Conclusion approach is one of the most effective ways to structure a proposal. It's simple clear and ensures your message resonates with the audience. It works like this:

1. The Opening: Introduce, connect, and set the stage

The opening of your presentation sets the tone for everything that follows. It's your chance to introduce yourself, make an emotional connection and set clear expectations for what's to come.

Key components of a strong opening

- **Who You Are.** Briefly introduce yourself and your team (if there are colleagues with you), emphasising your expertise and experience. For example: "*Good morning, I'm [Your Name], and I'm delighted to be here today to discuss how we can help [Customer*

Organisation] achieve [their objective]. With over [X years] of experience working with businesses like yours, we've had great success solving challenges just like the one we'll discuss today".

- **Make an emotional connection.** Share a positive statement that reflects your enthusiasm for the opportunity, while also paying a compliment to the customer. This builds rapport and demonstrates that you've taken the time to understand their business. For example: *"We're really excited about this opportunity, not only because of the impact we believe our solution can have but because [Customer Organisation] has such a strong reputation for [specific compliment—e.g., innovation, customer service, sustainability]. It's clear you're making a difference in your industry, and we'd love to be part of that".*

- **Set a clear call to action.** Tell the customer what you hope to achieve by the end of the presentation. Be specific about the next step. For example: *"Our objective today is to walk you through our proposal, demonstrate how it aligns with your objectives, and agree on the next steps to move forward."*

2. The Body: Present your solution and demonstrate value

The body of your presentation is where you "tell them." This is where you walk through the proposal, explain your solution in detail and connect it back to their specific objectives and challenges.

Tips for the body of your presentation.

- **Stick to the structure** from chapter 14 - follow the SOMQCB model (situation, objective, methodology, qualifications, cost, benefits) to ensure clarity and flow.

- **Engage your audience**: Don't just talk at them, engage them. Pause to ask questions such as: *"Does this align with what you were hoping to see?"* or *"Would you like me to expand on any of these steps?"*

- **Use storytelling**. Stories and real-life examples bring your solution to life and help customers visualise success. For example: *"We worked with a company facing similar* *challenges, and within six months, they saw a 20% improvement in operational efficiency".*

- **Address objections proactively**. If you anticipate concerns, address them naturally as part of the presentation rather than waiting for the customer to bring them up. This demonstrates confidence and preparedness. Use the APAC and FFF techniques described in the following chapter on "Handling Objections".

3. The conclusion: Summarise and call to action

The conclusion is where you "tell them what you told them." It's your opportunity to reinforce key points, remind the customer of the value you bring, and clearly articulate what happens next.

Key components of a strong conclusion:

- **Summarise the key benefits.** Restate how your solution aligns with their objectives and the measurable outcomes it delivers. To ensure focus and clarity, limit these objectives to their top three priorities.
- **Reiterate the call to action.** Close with a clear next step. Whether it's agreeing on a follow-up meeting, starting a trial, or reviewing the contract, make the next step easy and actionable.
- **End with confidence and gratitude.** Thank the customer for their time and express enthusiasm about working together.

A key point to remember here is that if you don't sound confident and enthusiastic about the opportunity, don't expect the customer to sound confident and enthusiastic about you and your proposal.

The 'presenter state'

Delivering a presentation is not just about the content, it's also about your mindset and presence. Mastering "the presenter state" will help you appear confident, connect with your audience and deliver your message effectively. Here are key elements to embody this state:

- **Own the Space**. Familiarise yourself with the presentation environment beforehand. If possible, visit the room in advance to understand the layout, lighting, and technology. This helps you feel more in control on the day

- **Practice makes perfect**. Don't let your first delivery be in front of your audience. Rehearse thoroughly to refine your timing, flow and delivery. Practice builds confidence and reduces nerves.
- **Make eye contact.** Engage with your audience by making eye contact with individuals. Speak to one person at a time to create a sense of connection and ensure your message resonates.
- **Stay present**. Focus fully on the moment and your message. Avoid distractions and centre your energy on communicating clearly and passionately
- **Know your stuff**. Be thoroughly familiar with your content. A strong grasp of your material ensures you can handle unexpected questions and maintain credibility
- **Keep it simple**. Speak conversationally, as if explaining to a friend. Avoid overloading your audience with jargon, acronyms or complex ideas
- **Utilise visuals effectively**. Ensure your visuals complement your presentation rather than distracting from it. They should enhance understanding, not compete for attention
- **Respect time limits**. Ensure your content fits within the allocated time, leaving space for questions. Pacing your delivery helps keep the audience engaged, (more on this to follow).
- **Anticipate questions**. Prepare answers to likely questions in advance. Being ready for audience inquiries demonstrates expertise and builds trust.
- **Clarify roles**. If presenting as part of a team, decide in advance who will present specific content and who will handle questions. Clear roles ensure a smooth delivery.

By embracing these elements, you'll establish confidence, foster engagement, and deliver a compelling presentation that leaves a lasting impression.

Researching your Audience

Understanding your audience is essential for tailoring your presentation to their needs and ensuring your message resonates. Thorough research allows you to connect meaningfully and deliver value. Here are key steps:

- **Identify your audience**. Determine who will be in the room. Understand their roles, decision-making power and level of knowledge about your topic.
- **Understand their needs and goals.** Research what matters most to your audience. What challenges do they face? How can your presentation address their priorities and provide solutions?

- **Gauge their knowledge level.** Assess how familiar your audience is with your subject. Avoid being overly technical for non-experts or oversimplifying for specialists.
- **Learn about their industry and trends.** Familiarise yourself with industry-specific challenges, terminology and trends. Demonstrating this understanding builds credibility and rapport.
- **Consider their expectations**. Understand what the audience expects to gain from your presentation. Whether it's insights, solutions or inspiration, tailor your content to meet these expectations.
- **Adapt to their communication style**. Consider how your audience prefers to receive information, visuals, data, storytelling or a mix. Align your presentation style with their preferences

By investing time in understanding your audience, you'll create a presentation that is relevant, engaging, and compelling, ultimately achieving stronger connections and better outcomes.

Time management

I've lost count of how many salespeople have presented to me over the years and not completed their presentations in the time allotted, here's some tips on how to avoid it happening to you.

- **Create a time plan**: Break your presentation into sections with time limits, including a buffer for Q&A or unexpected delays.
- **Practice and refine**: Rehearse with a timer to ensure you stay within your allotted time and adjust content if needed.
- **Prepare for questions**: Anticipate audience queries and plan how to address them effectively.
- **The car park**: If you feel you have lost control and a question or discussion has broken out that's killing your time, say this: *"In the interest of keeping on track with time, can we place this issue in the car park for now and return to it in more detail if you feel it isn't covered in the remainder of the presentation."*
- **Start on time**: Begin promptly and outline the agenda to set expectations.
- **Stay on track**: Focus on key points, monitor your time, and adjust if needed.
- **Conclude efficiently**: Summarise key points, provide a clear next step, and finish within the scheduled time.

Efficient time management keeps you to task and respects the customer's schedule. If you get this wrong you risk losing your audience before you deliver the key points of your proposal.

The importance of practicing your presentation

Great presentations rarely happen on the first attempt. They're the result of preparation and practice.

To deliver a polished, confident presentation:

- **Rehearse your delivery.** Practice the flow of your presentation, timing and transitions between sections.
- **Know your proposal inside out.** Be ready to answer questions and objections without fumbling or referring back to the document too often.
- **Coordinate roles**. If multiple team members are presenting, ensure everyone knows their part and who will handle specific questions or objections.
- **Record yourself.** If possible, record your practice presentation and review it to identify areas for improvement.

If you kid yourself into saying you don't have time to practice, then reconcile yourself with the fact that your first practice will be when you actually deliver it to the customer. If you get it wrong they will not invite you back to do it again.

The power of presentation

Presenting your proposal is your chance to bring your solution to life, engage with your customer, and move the sales process forward. By delivering it personally and following a clear Open-Body-Conclusion structure, you can create a professional, compelling experience that reassures the customer and inspires confidence.

Remember: your proposal presentation is not about theatrics, flashy slides or being a stand-up comedian. It's about connecting with the customer, demonstrating value, and setting a clear path forward. Approach it with preparation, professionalism and a strong call to action, and you'll turn your proposal into a powerful step toward winning the deal.

Warning on the use of comedy in B2B sales presentations

While a little humour can be a great way to connect with an audience, it must be used with extreme caution in a professional B2B sales environment. The purpose of your presentation is to convey value, build credibility and move the sales opportunity forward, not to entertain or amuse. If people want to see a comedian, they'll go to a comedy club, not a business meeting.

Besides, comedy can be risky, for these reasons:

- **Risk of misinterpretation:** Humour is subjective and what you find funny may not resonate with or could even offend your audience
- **Distraction from the message:** A poorly timed or irrelevant joke can shift focus away from the key points of your proposal.
- **Loss of credibility:** Excessive or inappropriate use of humour can undermine the seriousness of your message, leading the audience to question your expertise.

This is not to say your presentation should be dour or humourless. Adding a touch of warmth, positivity, and relatability is encouraged. A light-hearted remark or a friendly anecdote, provided it's relevant and appropriate, can help you connect with your audience. However, these moments should enhance your presentation, not overshadow it.

How to incorporate humour

- **Keep it subtle and relevant:** A light comment tied to your industry, audience, or proposal can add personality without disrupting professionalism.
- **Know your audience:** Only use humour if you are confident it aligns with the audience's culture and preferences.
- **Test it in practice:** Run any humorous elements by colleagues during rehearsal to gauge their reaction and ensure appropriateness.

Deliver your best presentation

Remember, your audience expects a professional, engaging experience that demonstrates your understanding of their needs and presents a clear solution. Focus on clarity, confidence, and delivering value and you'll leave a lasting positive impression without the risk of misplaced jokes derailing your efforts.

Exercise: Customer presentation role play

To improve your ability to present proposals effectively, engage in a practical role-play exercise that simulates a real presentation environment.

Exercise steps

1. **Set the scenario** Create a mock scenario based on a real or hypothetical customer situation. Include:

   - Customer background (industry, challenges, and objectives).
   - Proposal details (solutions, costs, and expected outcomes).
   - Colleagues or peers to act as the customer audience.

2. **Prepare your presentation**

   - Use the Open-Body-Conclusion structure to organize your content.
   - Prepare visuals and supporting materials if applicable.
   - Anticipate customer-specific questions and objections.

3. **Deliver your presentation**

   - Present your proposal to the mock audience as you would to a real customer.
   - Focus on making an emotional connection, maintaining eye contact, and managing your time.

4. **Simulate real-time interaction**

   - Encourage the mock audience to ask questions or raise objections during the presentation.
   - Practice addressing these concerns confidently and staying on track and on time.

5. **Get feedback**

   - Ask the audience to provide constructive feedback on your delivery, clarity, and engagement.
   - Specifically request input on your ability to connect with the audience, address objections, and stay within the time limit.

6. **Refine and repeat**

- Use the feedback to identify areas for improvement.
- Repeat the exercise, incorporating changes to enhance your presentation skills.

Reflection

This role-play exercise allows you to simulate a high-stakes environment in a low-risk setting, enabling you to refine your approach and build confidence. By consistently practicing, you'll develop the ability to deliver polished, impactful presentations that resonate with customers and drive results.

It's an ideal activity for a sales team meeting. In advance of the meeting inform everyone attending that someone will be asked to present for 10 minutes on a specific topic such as a business matter or a general topic (for example, the benefits of using public transport).

At the meeting, put everyone's name on a piece of paper, fold them, mix them up and select a presenter. This way if you have 10 people attending, they will have all prepared, even though only one presents.

Chapter 16: Objection handling: Turning challenges into opportunities

"An objection is not a rejection; it is simply a request for more information." – Zig Ziglar.

In B2B sales, objections are an inevitable part of the process. Far from being roadblocks, they are often a sign of genuine interest, a signal that your customer is engaged and seriously evaluating your solution. However, objections can feel daunting if you aren't prepared to address them confidently and constructively.

The key to handling objections successfully is preparation, active listening and a problem-solving mindset. Anticipating objections and crafting responses ahead of time allows you to navigate these conversations smoothly and maintain control of the sales process.

In this chapter I'll delve into practical strategies for handling objections and explore the psychology behind them, offering insights into why they occur and how to address them effectively. By understanding the emotional and cognitive drivers of objections, you can turn challenges into opportunities for building trust and advancing the sale.

Why objections are a good thing. Objections may initially feel like barriers, but they are a natural part of the buying process and often signal progress. Here's why objections matter:

- **They indicate interest:** If a customer raises objections, it usually means they're seriously evaluating your solution. Without interest, they'd likely disengage rather than voice concerns.
- **They uncover concerns:** Objections reveal specific areas where the customer needs reassurance or clarification. Understanding their concerns enables you to tailor your response effectively.
- **They move the sale forward:** Successfully addressing objections builds trust, demonstrates your expertise and removes barriers to closing the deal.

Objections often arise from fear of change or perceived risk. Customers need reassurance that adopting your solution will lead to positive outcomes.

The psychology behind objections

Understanding the psychology of objections can help you address them more effectively. Objections are rarely just about the surface issue; they are often rooted in deeper emotional and cognitive processes. By identifying these drivers, you can tailor your approach to address the true underlying concerns. Here are common psychological drivers behind objections.

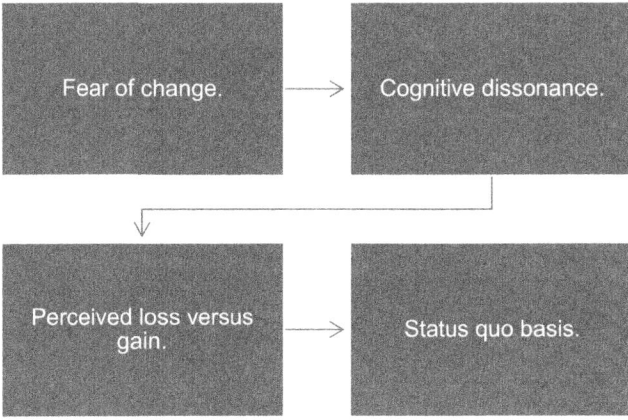

Fear of change

Change is inherently uncomfortable for most people. Customers may worry about the disruption a new solution might bring, fear unknown outcomes or feel anxious about their ability to adapt. This resistance can manifest as objections like, "We've always done it this way," or "I'm not sure if we're ready for this."

How to Address It

- **Empathise:** Acknowledge that change can be daunting. For instance:
  "I understand that moving away from your current system might feel like a big step. Many of our clients initially felt the same but found the transition smoother than expected with our support." This is the feel, felt, found technique. We will cover it in more detail later in the chapter.
- **Provide reassurance:** Share examples of other customers who successfully navigated similar changes and highlight the support you offer during the transition.

Cognitive dissonance

Cognitive dissonance occurs when people experience a conflict between their current beliefs and the actions they are considering. For example, a customer might want to solve a pressing problem but may be hesitant about committing resources - similar to wanting to lose weight but not wanting to change eating habits.

How to address it:

- **Align with their objectives:** Reaffirm their commitment to solving the problem and help them see how the action aligns with their values. For example: *"You mentioned earlier that improving efficiency is a top priority for your team. Our solution aligns directly with that objective and can help you achieve measurable results quickly."*
- **Simplify the decision:** Break the process into smaller, manageable steps. Offering a pilot program or phased implementation can help ease the dissonance.

Perceived loss vs. gain

People tend to focus more on potential losses (time, money, effort) than on potential gains, a cognitive bias known as loss aversion. Even when the benefits of a solution outweigh the costs, the fear of losing something tangible can hold customers back.

How to address it:

- **Quantify the gains:** Use data to show the long-term benefits and ROI of your solution. *"By automating this process, you'll save an estimated £50,000 annually in operational costs, far outweighing the initial investment."*
- **Minimise the risk:** Offer guarantees, flexible payment plans or trial periods to mitigate their sense of loss.
- **Inspire action:** For those who enjoy personal development, recommend the books, "Who Moved My Cheese" by Spencer Johnson or "Leading Change" by John P. Kotter which both explore overcoming resistance to change excellently.

Status quo bias

Customers may prefer sticking to familiar methods, even if they are less effective. The comfort of the status quo can lead to objections like, "What we have now works fine" or "We're managing okay without it."

How to address it

- **Highlight the cost of inaction:** Frame your solution as a way to avoid potential pitfalls or missed opportunities. *"If you don't take any steps to increase the sales team's capability, the outlook is that their results are highly unlikely to improve."*

- **Introduce a vision of the future:** Paint a compelling picture of what success could look like with your solution in place. *"Imagine reducing your reporting time by 50%, freeing your team to focus on strategic projects instead of manual tasks".*
- **Use comparisons:** Share case studies or testimonials that showcase how similar organisations have successfully transitioned from the status quo to your solution.

Building confidence through psychology with the APAC model

By recognising the psychological drivers behind objections, you can craft responses that reduce uncertainty and build trust. The APAC Model, Acknowledge, Probe, Address, Confirm provides a structured approach to handle objections effectively and foster confidence.

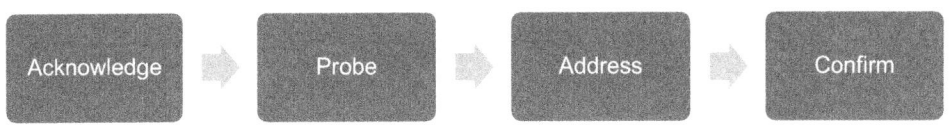

1. **Acknowledge the Concern**

The first step is to validate the customer's feelings and show empathy. Acknowledging their concern helps diffuse tension and demonstrates that you're listening. Here's a classic opening for this technique.

"I completely understand why you might feel uncertain about the timeline. It's a significant decision and it's natural to have questions."

This step reassures the customer that their objection is valid, worthy of consideration and that you are listening to them.

2. **Probe for underlying issues**

Dig deeper to uncover the root cause of the objection. Often, the stated concern is a surface-level expression of a deeper worry. Ask questions like:

- *"Can you tell me more about why this timeline feels tight? Are there specific deadlines you're working towards?"*
- *"You mentioned concerns about cost. Could you elaborate on how this fits into your budget priorities?"*

Probing helps clarify the true objection, allowing you to address it with precision.

3. Address the concern with evidence

Once you fully understand the objection, respond with tailored solutions and supporting evidence. This step builds credibility and reduces uncertainty.

Use data, success stories, or real-world examples to support your response:

- *"I understand your concern about cost. Many clients initially hesitated, but after implementing this solution, they saw a 20% reduction in operational expenses within six months. I'd be happy to share a case study that illustrates this."*

Simplify decision-making by breaking complex decisions into smaller steps:

- *"If the full implementation feels like too much right now, we could start with a pilot program to test the impact before committing fully."*

By aligning your response with their priorities, you make it easier for the customer to see the value of your solution.

4. Confirm resolution and next steps

After addressing the objection, confirm that the customer feels reassured and move the conversation forward.

"Does that address your concern about the timeline? If so, we can outline a phased plan that aligns with your priorities"?

This step ensures that the objection has been fully resolved and transitions the discussion toward the next phase of the decision-making process.

Why the APAC model works

The APAC model leverages psychological principles to build trust and reduce resistance:

- Acknowledging the concern shows empathy, which fosters trust.
- Probing uncovers the real issue, ensuring you're addressing the true objection.
- Addressing with evidence reduces uncertainty and reinforces your credibility.

- Confirming ensures clarity and allows you to close the loop, guiding the conversation forward.

By applying this model, you not only resolve objections effectively but also strengthen your relationship with the customer, paving the way for successful outcomes.

The 'Feel, Felt, Found' framework

The Feel, Felt, Found technique, popularised by Zig Ziglar, is a timeless method for addressing objections with empathy, relatability, and resolution. It aligns seamlessly with the APAC model by providing a conversational framework that acknowledges concerns, probes deeper and addresses them effectively. Outlined below is how the model works.

- **Feel**: Acknowledge the customer's objection and empathise with their concern. This step aligns with the Acknowledge phase of the APAC Model, demonstrating that you've heard and understood their feelings. *"I understand how you feel. It's natural to have concerns about the upfront cost of a solution like this."*
- **Felt**: Relate their objection to the experiences of others who had similar concerns. This step reflects the Probe phase by subtly exploring the underlying concern while introducing relatability. *"Many of our customers initially felt the same way, they were worried about committing to the investment"*.
- **Found**: Provide a resolution by sharing what others discovered after moving forward. This step ties to the Address and Confirm phases of the APAC Model, offering evidence and reassurance to resolve the objection. *"What they found was that the solution paid for itself within six months, thanks to the significant cost savings and increased efficiency it delivered"*.

Feel, Felt, Found in action

We've already incorporated elements of the Feel, Felt, Found technique in several examples throughout this chapter. For instance, in handling price objections, we used language like:

- *"I understand that budget is a concern. Many of our clients felt the same way initially, but they found that the ROI far outweighed the initial investment, with cost savings of 20% in the first year."*

By combining Feel, Felt, Found with the APAC model, you can create a more dynamic and empathetic approach to objection handling. This dual framework allows you to address both the emotional and logical components of objections, making your responses more persuasive and effective.

Key principles of handling objections

- Stay calm and confident: Don't get defensive or flustered. Confidence reassures the customer that you can address their concerns
- Listen fully before responding: Let the customer express their objection completely. Interrupting or rushing to defend your solution can make them feel unheard. Use active listening techniques to confirm their concern
- Ask questions to understand: Dig deeper into the objection to uncover its root cause. Often, objections are surface-level statements masking deeper concerns.
- Respond with value: Align your response with the customer's priorities and goals. Focus on how your solution addresses their specific needs and pain points.
- Confirm and move forward: Once you've addressed the objection, confirm the resolution and gently advance the conversation. "Does that address your concern? If so, let's revisit how this solution aligns with your goals".

Advanced strategies for handling objections

As you become more adept at handling objections, integrating advanced techniques can elevate your effectiveness. These methods go beyond standard responses, allowing you to connect more deeply with the customer, shift their perspective and engage them in collaborative solutions. Here are four advanced strategies to incorporate into your objection-handling toolkit.

1. Empathy mapping

Empathy mapping involves visualising the customer's perspective, emotions and objectives to better understand their concerns. By stepping into their shoes, you can anticipate objections and frame your responses in a way that resonates with their unique situation. Application: *"It sounds like you're worried about the upfront cost because of limited budget flexibility this quarter. Let's explore how we can make this work within your constraints while addressing your immediate needs."*

2. Reframing techniques

Reframing is about shifting the customer's mindset by presenting their objection in a new light. For example, instead of seeing "too expensive" as a dead-end, turn it into a discussion about ROI and the long-term value your solution delivers.

Application: *"I understand this feels like a significant investment. What if we focus on the return you'll see within the first year, like the 20% reduction in operational costs (or the 15% increase in closed deals or the improved Trust Pilot ratings) our other clients have experienced?"*

3. The power of silence

Silence can be an incredibly powerful tool in conversations. After addressing an objection, pause deliberately to give the customer space to reflect or elaborate. Often, they'll provide additional insights or even talk themselves into seeing your perspective.

4. Collaborative problem-solving

Involving the customer in resolving their objection fosters a sense of ownership and partnership. This approach shifts the dynamic from adversarial to collaborative, where both sides work toward a mutually beneficial outcome.

Application: *"It sounds like the timeline is tight. What if we explore a phased approach that allows us to address your highest priorities first and expand as your schedule permits?"*

These advanced strategies allow you to address objections with sophistication, empathy and creativity. By using empathy mapping, reframing techniques, silence, and collaborative problem-solving, you can create a more engaging and persuasive conversation that not only resolves concerns but also builds trust and rapport.

Always try to remember, objection handling is not about winning an argument, it's about guiding the customer towards a solution that aligns with their objectives and priorities. By mastering these techniques, you position yourself as a trusted advisor who not only understands their concerns but also empowers them to overcome barriers and make confident decisions.

Preparing for common objections

Anticipating potential objections allows you to craft thoughtful, confident responses that demonstrate your expertise and keep the sales conversation moving forward. Below are common objections I've encountered in B2B sales and tactics for addressing each one confidently.

1. Price or budget

Objection: "It's too expensive" or "We don't have the budget for this right now".

What it means

Price objections often indicate that the customer hasn't yet perceived the full value of your solution or how it aligns with their priorities. In some cases, it may reflect genuine budget constraints.

How to address it

- Shift the focus to ROI: Demonstrate how your solution will deliver measurable returns, such as cost savings, revenue growth or the intrinsic value of increased brand perception.
  "I understand that budget is a concern, but if the sales training helps you sell two more networks next quarter this solution will pay for itself."
- Offer flexible options: Explore phased implementations, payment plans or scaled-down versions to fit their budget.
  "If the full implementation feels like too much right now, we can start with the core modules and expand as you see results."
- Use social proof: Share case studies or testimonials from customers who initially hesitated on price but later achieved significant ROI.
  "One of our clients in a similar position was able to save £50,000 annually with this solution. I'd be happy to share their story or put you in touch with them."

2. Timing

Objection: "The timing isn't right," or "Let's revisit this in six months".

What it means

Timing objections often stem from competing priorities, uncertainty about the urgency of the solution or the perception that this isn't the right moment to act.

How to address it

- Create a sense of urgency: Emphasise the cost or risk of inaction to help the customer see the benefits of acting now.
- *"I understand timing is important, but have you considered the potential impact of leaving this challenge unresolved for another six months? Operational inefficiencies could cost significantly more than the initial investment in this solution."*
- Align with their priorities: Ask questions to understand their current priorities and explore how your solution can address them.
  "Can you share what's taking precedence right now? Perhaps we can tailor the solution to accommodate your most immediate needs."
- Suggest an incremental step: Propose a pilot program or phased approach to allow them to experience the benefits without full commitment.
  "How about we start with a smaller-scale implementation? That way, you can see the results firsthand before making a larger investment".

3. Fit or relevance

Objection: "I'm not sure this solution is right for us," or "We're already managing this internally."

What it means

This objection suggests that the customer may not fully understand how your solution aligns with their needs or believe it offers enough improvement over their current methods.

How to address it

- **Revisit their needs:** Confirm their key challenges and priorities to ensure alignment.
  "You mentioned earlier that improving efficiency is a priority. Can I show you how our solution directly addresses that?"
- **Tailor your value proposition:** Use specific examples to demonstrate how your solution meets their needs.
  "We've helped companies like yours reduce manual work by 30%, allowing their teams to focus on strategic projects. Would you like me to show how this could work for you?"
- **Offer a demonstration:** A demo or trial can provide clarity and allow them to experience the solution in action.
  "Would you be open to a quick demonstration? I think it'll help you see how this could fit seamlessly into your processes?"

4. Trust or credibility

Objection: *"We've never worked with your company before"* or *"How do I know this will work?"*

What it means

This objection reflects a lack of trust or familiarity with your company or product. The customer may need reassurance that you can deliver what you promise.

How to address it:

- Share case studies and testimonials: Provide examples of similar clients who achieved success with your solution.
  "We worked with [Client Name], who had similar concerns initially, and they've now seen a 25% increase in staff retention. I'd be happy to connect you with them to discuss their experience."
- Highlight your expertise: Emphasise your track record, experience, and industry knowledge.
  "We've been partnering with businesses in your sector for more than 10 years, and our clients typically see results within [timeframe]."
- Offer references or guarantees: Reassure them with references from satisfied customers or a performance guarantee if applicable.

5. Competition

Objection: "We're considering a similar solution from another provider".

What it means

The customer is evaluating alternatives and may be unsure how your solution compares. It may also be a blatant negotiation tactic to derail you, an aspect we will cover this in the next chapter.

How to address it

- Differentiate yourself: Highlight the unique aspects of your solution without disparaging competitors.

"We respect [Competitor], but one area in which we consistently hear that we stand out is our personalised onboarding and ongoing support."

- Focus on value: Emphasise the specific benefits your solution offers, such as superior ROI, better support, or scalability.

"What many of our clients find is that while there are other options, our solution provides a faster implementation timeline and a better long-term cost structure."

- Ask insightful questions: Gain insights into what they value most by asking about their evaluation criteria.

"What's most important to you when comparing solutions? Perhaps we can dive deeper into those aspects to help you decide."

Preparation and why it matters

Just as we have focused on preparation in many of the chapters of this book, preparing for common objections ensures you can respond confidently and effectively when they arise.

By addressing objections with thoughtful, tailored strategies, you not only overcome barriers but also position yourself as a flexible partner. Remember, objections are opportunities to demonstrate your expertise and help your customer make the best decision for their needs."

Exercise: Mastering objection handling

This exercise is designed to help you practice and develop the skills outlined in this chapter. By applying the models and techniques discussed, you can refine your ability to handle objections effectively and confidently in real-world scenarios.

Step 1: Identify common objections

Take 15 minutes with your colleagues to brainstorm the top five objections you encounter in your sales process. Use the categories discussed in the chapter as a starting point,

- Price or budget
- Timing
- Fit or relevance
- Trust or credibility
- Competition

For each objection, write down a brief explanation of why you believe it arises (fear of change, cognitive dissonance, perceived loss or status quo bias).

Step 2: Craft responses using the APAC model

For each objection, create a response following the APAC model:

- **Acknowledge:** Write a sentence that validates the customer's concern. Example: *"I completely understand why this feels like a significant investment. It's natural to weigh the costs carefully."*
- **Probe:** Write one or two questions to uncover the root cause of the objection. Example: *"Can you tell me more about how this fits into your budget priorities?"*
- **Address:** Create a response that provides evidence or a solution to resolve the concern. Example: *"Many of our clients initially hesitated, but they found that the ROI from increased efficiency paid for the investment within six months."*
- **Confirm:** Write a sentence to ensure the objection is resolved and move the conversation forward. Example: *"Does this address your concern? If so, we can outline the next steps to implement a phased approach."*

Step 3: Integrate the 'Feel, Felt, Found' technique

Select two of the objections from Step 1 and rewrite your responses using the Feel, Felt, Found framework.

- Feel: Acknowledge the objection with empathy. Example: *"I understand how you feel. It's natural to have concerns about the upfront cost of a solution like this"*.
- Felt: Relate the objection to the experiences of others. Example: *"Many of our clients initially felt the same way—they were worried about committing to the investment"*.
- Found: Share what others discovered after moving forward. Example: *"What they found was that the solution paid for itself within six months, thanks to significant cost savings and increased efficiency"*.

Step 4: Role play scenarios

Partner with a colleague, mentor or friend to role-play objection-handling scenarios. Take turns playing the customer and the salesperson.

- As the customer, present one of the objections you wrote in Step 1. Add realistic emotional elements, such as hesitation or uncertainty.
- As the salesperson, use the APAC model and/or Feel, Felt, Found technique to handle the objection.
- Provide feedback to each other on what worked well and what could be improved.

If you're working alone, record yourself handling each objection and review your responses critically.

Step 5: Analyse real-world interactions

In your next sales conversations, actively apply the APAC model and Feel, Felt, Found framework. Afterward, reflect on the following:

Which objections arose?

- How did you address them?
- What worked well, and what could have been improved?
- Did the customer's concern feel resolved?

Document your observations to track your progress over time.

This exercise encourages both theoretical preparation and practical application. By identifying common objections, crafting thoughtful responses, and practicing in realistic scenarios, you will build confidence and mastery in objection handling.

Remember, objection handling is a skill that improves with consistent practice and reflection. Over time, you'll develop an instinct for navigating objections smoothly, turning them into opportunities to strengthen your customer relationships and close more deals.

Chapter 17: Negotiation

"In any negotiation, the most important thing to remember is that you are negotiating with a person, not a position" – Anonymous.

Negotiation is a critical part of the B2B sales process and it often represents the final stretch before closing a deal. In the simplest terms, negotiation is about finding a mutually beneficial outcome, a win-win where both parties feel confident and satisfied with the agreement.

However, negotiation can be a challenging phase, particularly in high-stakes or complex sales opportunities. Customers may push back on price, terms or scope, and salespeople often face pressure to concede too quickly or compromise on value. The key to successful negotiation lies in preparation, understanding the customer's priorities, personality types (as covered in earlier chapters) and robust opportunity qualification, combined with using proven techniques to navigate the negotiation process confidently.

In this chapter, I'll explore practical negotiation strategies, how to recognise and respond to common tactics and how the Thomas-Kilmann Conflict Model can help you adapt your negotiation approach, based on the particular negation scenario you are faced with.

Let's begin with a look at a few negotiation basics.

What is a negotiation?

Negotiation can be defined as "a discussion aimed at reaching an agreement" (Oxford English Dictionary). This succinct definition encapsulates the essence of all negotiation scenarios, regardless of their complexity. Whether the matter at hand is as straightforward as agreeing on the price of a product or as intricate as finalising a high-value complex sales opportunity, the core principle remains the same. You and whoever you are negotiating with engage in dialogue to find common ground.

In practice, negotiations are rarely one-off, high-stakes encounters filled with tension as they are often portrayed. While such scenarios do occur, most negotiations unfold as iterative, multi-stage processes. This is particularly true in professional or commercial contexts, where negotiations resemble the sales process, characterised by ongoing exchanges, adjustments and mutual concessions.

An effective negotiation builds gradually through the sales process, fostering collaboration and understanding, while gradually moving toward a resolution. The key to effective negotiation lies in maintaining this momentum, ensuring that all parties feel valued and that their concerns are addressed. Recognising negotiation as a dynamic, evolving process helps you approach discussions with patience, flexibility and a focus on long-term outcomes.

Why negotiations happen

Negotiation typically arises for three main reasons, each highlighting a unique need for dialogue and agreement between two (or more) parties.

First, negotiations occur to determine how to share or divide limited resources, such as land, money, access or time. These situations involve finding equitable solutions where resources are constrained, requiring compromise and collaboration.

Second, negotiations are necessary to create something new that neither party could achieve independently. By pooling ideas, resources or expertise, parties can innovate and build opportunities that benefit all involved.

Finally, negotiation is a vital tool for resolving problems or disputes. Whether addressing interpersonal conflicts, contractual disagreements or complex societal issues, negotiation enables parties to find common ground and move forward constructively.

In essence, negotiation is a versatile process that facilitates agreement, creativity, and resolution, adapting to diverse contexts and needs while fostering mutual understanding and progress. Furthermore, it's going on all around us, all the time.

Negotiation in everyday life

Many of us think of negotiation as something reserved for boardrooms or legal settings, but in reality, most of us negotiate daily without even realising it.

Consider deciding where to go on holiday with a partner. Balancing preferences, budgets, and timing can be a negotiation in itself. Parents, too, often find themselves negotiating with their children, whether it's about bedtime, healthy eating, or screen time limits. Children, in fact, are master negotiators, relentlessly persistent, even if not always sensible. Witness the way they can argue for "just five more minutes" or an extra treat with remarkable skill.

Other examples include discussing household chores, agreeing on social plans with friends or managing shared spaces with roommates. At work, you might negotiate deadlines, workloads, or project responsibilities. From big decisions to seemingly minor compromises, negotiation is woven into the fabric of our daily lives, highlighting its universal importance as a skill worth mastering.

The Thomas-Kilmann conflict model in negotiation

Negotiation often involves navigating different levels of conflict, where you and the customer may have competing priorities. The Thomas-Kilmann conflict model provides a framework for understanding and adapting your approach to negotiation based on the situation.

The model identifies four styles of conflict management:

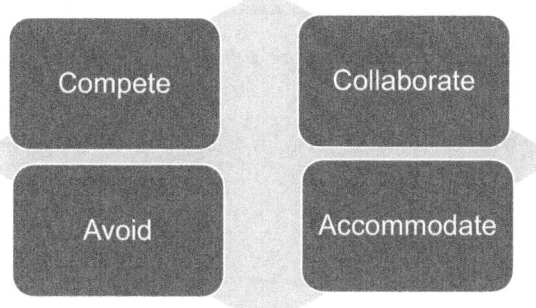

1. Compete: focused on winning

This assertive approach is about standing your ground and prioritising your needs over compromise.

When to use it

- When quick decisions are required, such as under tight deadlines.
- When key issues are non-negotiable and critical to maintaining value.

Example
"I understand your concerns, but we cannot compromise on these terms as they're critical to ensuring the solution delivers on its promise."

Risks

Overusing this style can create tension, damage relationships or make you appear inflexible. Use it sparingly to preserve long-term trust.

2. Collaborate: finding win-win solutions

Collaboration involves seeking solutions that meet the needs of both sides, fostering mutual satisfaction and long-term trust.

When to use it:

- When both parties have significant priorities and a mutually beneficial resolution is possible.
- For long-term relationships where trust and shared value are paramount.

Examples:
"Let's work together to find a solution that addresses your concerns while maintaining the value of what we're offering."
"If we adjust the timeline slightly, would that help meet your budget constraints?"

Risks:
Collaboration requires time and effort. In high-pressure situations, it may not be practical.

3. Avoid: stepping back temporarily

Avoidance means taking a step back from the issue to cool down emotions or gather additional information.

When to use it

- When emotions are running high, and progress is unlikely without a pause.
- When the issue is minor or inconsequential.

Risks

Avoiding conflict for too long can stall progress and harm credibility. Ensure you revisit the issue promptly to maintain momentum.

4. Accommodate: yielding to the customer

This cooperative style involves putting the other party's needs first, even at the expense of your own, to preserve the relationship.

When to use it

- When the relationship is more valuable than the immediate outcome.
- When the customer's ask is minor and easy to resolve.

Risks

Overusing accommodation can erode your value and weaken your position over time.

Final thoughts on the Thomas-Kilmann conflict model

Each style has its place in negotiation but understanding when and how to use them is key. Flexibility in adapting your approach to the situation, customer and priorities ensures better outcomes and stronger relationships. Negotiation isn't just about winning; it's about finding the right balance between value, relationships and outcomes.

Key negotiation terminology: ZOPA, BATNA, LAO, and BPO

Mastering negotiation terminology is essential for sales people navigating complex B2B deals. These concepts, named ZOPA, BATNA, LAO, and BPO are not just theoretical ideas. They are practical tools that give structure and clarity to the negotiation process. Understanding them allows you to approach discussions confidently, avoid unfavourable outcomes and maintain control.

ZOPA: zone of possible agreement

The Zone of Possible Agreement (ZOPA) is the range where both parties' needs overlap and an agreement is achievable. Without a ZOPA, a deal is unlikely because your and your customer's expectations are misaligned.

How it works

To identify the ZOPA, you must understand both your boundaries and the customer's. This requires knowing:

- Your acceptable range: Your minimum acceptable terms and your ideal outcome

- The customer's acceptable range: What the customer is prepared to accept or commit to, including price, scope, and timing.

For example, you price your services at £60,000-£80,000. The customer's budget is £50,000-£75,000. Here, there is clearly a ZOPA at the bottom end of your range and the top end of the customer's. If you anchor the discussion within this range and focus on the customer's priorities, perhaps highlighting ROI or specific features you increase the likelihood of agreement.

If the customer's budget or expectations fall outside your acceptable range, you must either reshape the discussion (by emphasising value) or accept that there may be no ZOPA. Walking away is better than wasting time and resources on making a deal that doesn't align with your objectives.

BATNA: best alternative to a negotiated agreement

Your BATNA is your "Plan B", the best alternative available if no agreement is reached. It's the fallback option that prevents you from making desperate or unfavourable concessions during negotiations.

Why BATNA matters

Knowing your BATNA gives you confidence. It allows you to say "no" to a bad deal because you understand there's another viable option.

For example, you're negotiating with a prospective client who insists on a 30% discount. Your BATNA is a strong pipeline with two other prospects who value your solution at full price. With this knowledge, you can calmly reject the discount and hold firm on value, knowing you have alternatives.

How to strengthen your BATNA:

- Maintain a healthy pipeline. A strong BATNA comes from having other viable opportunities.
- Explore other prospects or solutions internally before negotiations.
- Know what walking away looks like for your business.

Your BATNA may also involve protecting existing customers or refocusing efforts on accounts where your value is more appreciated. Always enter negotiations with clarity on what your fallback looks like.

LAO: least acceptable offer

The least acceptable offer is the minimum set of terms you're willing to accept while still achieving your business objectives. Anything below this threshold should result in walking away.

Why LAO matters

Defining your LAO prevents emotional decision-making under pressure. It ensures you don't agree to unfavourable terms that compromise profitability or credibility.

For example: Your company requires a 20% minimum margin on deals. A customer insists on terms that would result in a 15% margin. Since this breaches your LAO, you politely decline: *"I appreciate your position, but at that level, we wouldn't be able to deliver the level of service and value you expect."*

Practical application

- Before negotiations, define your LAO clearly and discuss it internally with stakeholders.
- Prepare alternatives (BATNA) in case the customer can't meet your minimum requirements.

BPO: best possible outcome

Understanding and defining your BPO (best possible outcome) is critical for setting clear goals and maximising value in any negotiation. Here's how you can apply the concept effectively.

Define the BPO beforehand
Before negotiations, collaborate with stakeholders to establish your BPO. Outline your ideal outcomes in terms of pricing, contract duration, timelines and any value-added components. This preparation ensures everyone is aligned on what success looks like.

Create anchoring points

Your BPO serves as an anchor that guides your opening offer. Starting with a strong yet reasonable proposal ensures you create room for negotiation while keeping your ideal outcome in sight.

Use the BPO to steer conversations

Frame your discussions to align with achieving your BPO. For example: *"We believe this proposal offers the best value for your investment while meeting your key priorities. Let's explore how we can finalize it in a way that benefits both sides."*

Stay flexible but strategic

While the BPO is your ideal result, remain open to adjustments within the ZOPA (Zone of Possible Agreement). Flexibility ensures progress and allows for creative solutions.

Evaluate progress against the BPO

During the negotiation process, compare offers to your BPO. If concessions are required, ensure they don't compromise your core objectives.

For example, your BPO is a 3-year, £80,000 contract with full implementation fees covered. You propose this during the negotiation but encounter resistance. By staying focused and flexible, you secure a £75,000 deal with partial implementation fees. While not the full BPO, it remains a strong outcome aligned with your objectives.

Practical application

- Clearly define the BPO with input from stakeholders.
- Use it as a guide to structure offers and discussions.
- Remain flexible to achieve the best result within realistic constraints.

A tale of two negotiations

The unreasonable demand

While working for Virgin Media, I encountered a customer who was moving their operations to a new location and demanded we fund the reinstallation of hundreds of communication circuits, a significant and unreasonable expense.

While we firmly declined to cover the costs, we worked creatively to retain their business. We proposed extending the length of their overall contract with us at a slightly reduced price, but they carried the costs of the re-installation at their new location.

This solution provided more revenue and profit for Virgin Media, while also increasing the customer's total return on investment over the full length of the contract. The customer appreciated the compromise and the extended partnership proved mutually beneficial.

Lesson learned: Even when faced with unreasonable demands, creative solutions and a focus on shared benefits can preserve relationships and achieve long-term gains.

The missed budget

During my time at Case Communications, I pitched a £1.2m solution to a customer who had made it clear from the outset that they had a strict £1m budget. I believed the additional value of our offering would justify the higher cost, so I pressed ahead without fully listening to their constraints. Unfortunately, the customer did not see it the same way, and I lost the deal entirely.

Lesson learned: Listening is paramount in negotiation. Ignoring a customer's explicit parameters can derail trust and cost valuable opportunities. Always tailor solutions to meet stated needs and constraints before trying to upsell.

BPO, LAO, ZOPA and BATNA in action

Imagine you're buying or selling a second-hand car. Your LAO, ZOPA and BPO framework, might look like the diagram below and your BATNA might be to lease a new car (minimal capital outlay) or buy an alternative vehicle or use public transport, (lower total cost of ownership). The dynamics are laid out in the diagram below.

Best Possible				Least Acceptable		Seller's Best Alternative to a Negotiated Agreement (BATNA)
Seller's Desired Negotiation Outcomes						
£10K	£9.5K	£9K	£7K	£6.5K	£6K	
Price			Zone of Potential Agreement			
Buyer's Best Alternative to a Negotiated Agreement (BATNA)			£7K	£6.5K	£6K	£5K	£4.5K	£4K
			Buyer's Desired Negotiation Outcomes					
			Least Acceptable					Best Possible

As you can see unless a deal can be made between £6k and £7k, both parties will be activating their BATNA.

Negotiation sources of power

In any negotiation, power is not just about dominance; it's about understanding and leveraging the factors that can influence the outcome. Power in negotiation stems from multiple sources, each affecting your ability to shape discussions and achieve favourable terms. Recognising these sources empowers you to maximise your position while remaining strategic and adaptable. Here are key sources of power and how to use them effectively with real-world examples.

1. Situational need: who needs whom the most?

The party that least needs the deal often holds the upper hand. If the customer is heavily reliant on your solution and has limited alternatives, this increases your leverage.

Example
A customer urgently needs a communication system upgrade before a regulatory deadline. Knowing their dependency, you can maintain your pricing while offering a timeline that fits their need.

Tip: Always assess dependency dynamics and position yourself as indispensable by highlighting the unique value you bring.

2. Influence: trust, relationships, and perception

Strong relationships and trust create power by making your counterpart more open to collaboration. Your reputation, credibility and perceived expertise also significantly impacts your influence.

Example
You've nurtured a strong relationship with a client over years, consistently delivering exceptional results. When entering negotiations for a new project, your established trust allows you to propose terms confidently, knowing they see you as a reliable partner.

Tip: Invest in building trust and rapport before negotiations begin. Influence is often earned long before the deal is on the table.

3. Time constraints: who is under more pressure?

Time can be a critical factor in negotiations. The party with less urgency typically has more room to manoeuvre.

Example:
A supplier facing an end-of-quarter sales target offers you favourable terms to close the deal quickly. Knowing their time pressure, you secure additional value by agreeing to their deadline.

Tip: Be aware of time constraints on both sides and avoid showing urgency unless it benefits your position.

Note: this is the reason most B2B sales happen in the last week of the month and the last month of a quarter. If you're ever buying a car, go to the showroom on the last Sunday of the quarter and you'll get the best deal.

4. Market conditions: seller's or buyer's market?

The state of the market can dictate power dynamics. In scarce markets, sellers hold the advantage; in abundant markets, buyers do.

Example:
In a niche market with limited competitors, you can justify premium pricing because the customer has few alternatives. Conversely, in a saturated market, you may need to differentiate through value-added benefits.

Tip: Research the market thoroughly to understand where the power lies and position your offer accordingly.

5. Future opportunity: one-off or long-term potential?

If a deal represents the potential for a long-term partnership or additional opportunities, it can significantly affect negotiation dynamics.

Example:
A client indicates this contract is a test for a much larger rollout across their organization. You decide to offer slightly more favourable terms upfront to secure the relationship and open the door for future business.

Tip: Always qualify robustly the long-term potential of a deal and tailor your approach to balance short-term value with future gains.

Final thoughts on power

Power in negotiation is rarely absolute. It's dynamic, situational and often subject to perception. By understanding these sources of power, situational need, influence, time constraints, market conditions and future opportunity, you can strategically navigate discussions to achieve win-win outcomes while maintaining control over the negotiation process.

Top 10 negotiation techniques you're likely to encounter and how to handle them

Negotiation is a game of strategy and tactics. As a salesperson, you'll encounter various techniques designed to extract concessions, test your resolve, or delay decisions. Over the years, I've encountered a wide range of these techniques and here are the top 10 that have been used on me, along with their purpose and my advice on how to respond effectively to maintain control and achieve positive outcomes.

1. The "higher authority" tactic

What is it?
The customer says, "I need to check with my boss/board/committee before deciding." It delays the process and is often used to extract further concessions.

How to handle it?

- Ask clarifying questions: "What feedback do you expect to get from them?"
- Identify all decision-makers early in the sales process.
- Offer support: "Would it help if I joined the next discussion to address any concerns they might have?"
- "Great, can we go see them now while I'm here"? (Use this with confident decision-makers).

2. The "nibble" technique

What is it?
After an agreement is reached, the customer asks for an additional concession, like a discount or added feature.

How to handle it?

- Push back respectfully: "The terms we agreed on reflect the value and benefits we've discussed."
- If you concede, trade: "I can include that, but could we finalise the agreement today?"
- Remember the mantra that, "nothing is agreed until everything is agreed."

3. The "good cop, bad cop" tactic

What is it?
One person is supportive and understanding ("good cop"), while the other applies pressure ("bad cop").

How to handle it?

- Stay calm and focused on the facts
- Address the "bad cop" with confidence: "I understand your concerns but let me clarify how our solution addresses your priorities."
- Reframe the discussion: Focus on mutual goals and outcomes.

4. Price objection or "that's too expensive"

What is it?
Customers push for a lower price, often using competitors' pricing as leverage.

How to handle it

- Reframe around value: "I understand budget concerns, but let's revisit the ROI this solution delivers."
- Prioritise: "What's more important, lowest cost, or achieving the outcomes we discussed?"
- Offer alternatives: adjust scope, timing, or terms rather than discounting your value.

An additional tip on this subject is when presenting your price, avoid undermining yourself with uncertain phrases like:

- "We usually charge…"
- "The recommended price is…"
- "Our standard price is…"

These expressions signal hesitation and invite the customer to push for discounts. Instead, confidently state your price along with a clear value statement. Once you've stated your price, resist the urge to ask, "How does that sound"?

This question opens the door for objections like, "That's too expensive". Let the customer process the offer and respond in their own time.

Your price must be credible and deliver clear value. If you've done your research and qualified the opportunity, you'll know if your price aligns with the customer's needs and expectations.

Before pitching, ask yourself: "Would I pay this price for the value offered?" If your answer isn't a confident yes, reevaluate your BPO and LAO to avoid a difficult conversation.

5. The "deadline pressure" tactic

What is it?
The customer applies time pressure to rush your decision, hoping for hasty concessions.

How to handle it?

- Slow down: "Let's take a moment to ensure we're making the best decision for both sides."
- Confirm their urgency: "Is there a specific reason for the deadline?"
- Use it to your advantage: "If timing is critical, let's finalise the agreement now to avoid delays."

6. Anchoring (unrealistic initial offers)

What is it?

The customer opens with an extreme or unrealistic offer to set a low baseline.

How to handle it?

- Counter anchor: "I appreciate your position, but based on market conditions, we're looking at something closer to X." Pitch this number at slightly (but not too much) over your BPO.
- Reframe expectations: "Let's focus on a solution that meets your goals within a realistic range."

7. Silence

What is it?

The customer remains silent after a proposal, hoping to make you uncomfortable enough to fill the void by conceding.

How to handle it

- Resist the urge to fill the silence. Stay confident and wait for their response.
- Use the silence to your advantage by calmly reiterating key points of value.

A tale of a coffee pot

I once found myself negotiating hard for a deal and at a pivotal moment, I asked the customer a direct question: "Are you prepared to sign today?" What followed was a tense silence that felt like an eternity, though it was probably only about 10 seconds.

On the 11th second, just as the customer was likely wrestling with their decision, a colleague (of mine) in the room heard the coffee percolator bubble. Breaking the silence, they blurted out, "Oh, the coffee's ready! Anyone fancy a brew?"

The customer immediately seized on the distraction, saying, "Oh yes, please," which completely defused the moment. The pressure to respond to my question vanished and the conversation shifted away from the decision I was driving toward.

Whilst I eventually closed the deal a week later, the momentum from that crucial moment was lost. There were no free coffees for my colleague after that.

Lesson learned: Silence is a powerful tool in negotiation. It creates space for the customer to reflect, process and decide. Never be afraid of silence, it often speaks louder than words. Most importantly, ensure your team is aligned on strategy and knows when to stay quiet, especially when the stakes are high.

8. The "split the difference" tactic

What is it?

A customer proposes splitting the difference between your offer and theirs as a compromise.

How to handle it

- Evaluate if it aligns with your objectives
- If conceding, trade: "I can agree to that, but let's also include X to ensure the deal remains balanced." This could be an up-sell or cross-sell.

A word of warning

Splitting the difference might seem like a fair compromise, but in negotiation, it can significantly erode your profitability. A reduction in price often leads to a disproportionate reduction in margin, especially when fixed costs remain unchanged.

For example, if your product has a 20% margin and you agree to split the difference on a £10,000 deal, reducing the price by 5% (£500), that £500 comes directly out of your profit. While it may seem minor, it represents a 25% reduction in your net margin, (from £2,000 to £1,500) not a small concession.

Additionally, splitting the difference can set a precedent, signalling to the customer that your initial price was inflated or negotiable. This undermines your perceived value and makes future negotiations more challenging.

Instead of conceding, focus on reinforcing the value of your offering. If a compromise is necessary, trade for something in return to protect your profitability and position.

9. The "red herring" tactic

What is it?

The customer focuses heavily on one issue (often minor) to distract you from more significant concessions elsewhere.

How to handle it

- Stay focused on the overall deal: "That's an important point, but let's make sure we're aligned on the bigger picture".
- Address the red herring briefly, then redirect to core priorities.

10. "Take it or leave it"

What is it?
The customer presents a final offer, suggesting no room for negotiation.

How to handle it?

- Test their resolve: "I understand where you're coming from. Would you be open to discussing this one last point to ensure the best outcome for both sides?"
- If necessary, walk away if it doesn't meet your LAO (least acceptable offer).

Recognising and preparing for these common negotiation techniques helps you maintain control, protect your value, and steer discussions toward win-win outcomes. Adapt your responses to the context, stay calm under pressure and always keep your LAO, BPO and BATNA in sight. These disciplines will help you handle even the most challenging negotiations with confidence.

The importance of preparation in negotiation

As with the other stages of the B2B sales cycle referred to in the other chapters, the cornerstone of any successful negotiation is preparation.

When you've done your homework, through effective qualification and a deep understanding of the customer's objectives and priorities, you enter negotiations with clarity, confidence and a strategy tailored to achieve the best outcomes. Preparation equips you to manage discussions effectively, navigate challenges and close deals that deliver mutual value.

Refer back to previous chapters on preparation to ensure that you understand the customer, anticipate objections, adapt to personality types – Dominant, Influential, Steady and Conscientious – and define your boundaries, your BATNA, LAO and of course your BPO.

Preparation transforms negotiations from reactive to proactive. By understanding your customer, anticipating challenges, adapting to personality types and setting clear boundaries, you position yourself to negotiate confidently and achieve outcomes that drive success.

Five practical tips for successful negotiation

- Prepare and practice: Know your value, your boundaries and your response to likely objections.
- Stay calm and professional: Never let negotiations become personal. Keep a level head.
- Focus on value, not just price: Tie every discussion back to how your solution meets their needs and delivers measurable results.
- Trade, don't concede: If you need to make concessions, ask for something in return. For example, faster decision timelines, reduced scope or extended contract length
- Know when to walk away: Not every deal is worth winning. If the terms undermine your value, it's okay to walk away respectfully.

Negotiation is not about "winning" at the customer's expense, it's about reaching an agreement that provides value for both sides. By preparing thoroughly you can approach negotiations with confidence and skill.

Using proven techniques, recognising common tactics and adapting your approach through frameworks like the Thomas-Kilmann model, you'll transform negotiation from a high-pressure standoff into a collaborative conversation. Done well, negotiation becomes another opportunity to reinforce your value, build trust, and move the deal toward a successful close.

A 30-minute exercise to improve negotiation skills

This exercise is designed to enhance your ability to handle negotiations confidently, adapt to different scenarios, and reinforce value-driven conversations.

Setup (5 minutes)

1. Choose a scenario - elect a common negotiation scenario you face in your role.

Examples:

- A customer makes an offer and says *"take it or leave it"*.
- The customer introduces the "higher authority" tactic.
- They compare your offering to a competitor's lower price.

2. Define roles:

- One person acts as the salesperson.
- Another acts as the customer (or objection-raising counterpart).
- If alone, write out the customer's objections and practice responding out loud.

3. Set the context: Agree on key details for the negotiation scenario, such as the product/service, price and customer priorities.

Exercise (20 minutes):

Step 1: Present the offer (3 minutes): The salesperson delivers their pitch confidently, including price, value, and benefits.

Step 2: Raise objections (10 minutes): The "customer" presents realistic objections aligned with the chosen scenario, such as:

- "Your competitor is offering a similar solution for 15% less."
- "I need more time to decide, this feels rushed."
- "We have a strict £10,000 budget and your proposal is £12,000."

The salesperson practices responding to these objections, focusing on:

- Reinforcing the value of the solution.
- Using strategic questioning to uncover priorities.
- Redirecting the conversation away from price toward outcomes.

Step 3: Feedback and reflection (5 Minutes)

The customer provides feedback on the salesperson's responses. Discuss what went well and identify areas for improvement.

- Write down one or two specific phrases or strategies to use in your next real negotiation.
- Repeat the exercise weekly, varying scenarios to build confidence in handling diverse objections.
- If working solo, reflect on your delivery – were your answers concise and confident? Did you effectively address the objections?

This exercise builds quick thinking, confidence and adaptability, essential skills for any B2B salesperson navigating high-stakes negotiations.

Chapter 18: Closing

"Always be closing" doesn't mean always be pressuring. It means always be aligning your solution to the client's needs." – Anonymous.

Have you ever watched a master closer at work? It's not about flashy words, dramatic gestures, or relentless pressure. Instead, it's a carefully orchestrated process, precision, timing and genuine connection, all coming together to guide a customer seamlessly toward a decision.

In the film Glengarry Glen Ross, Alec Baldwin's character delivers an unforgettable, no-holds-barred speech centred on the mantras of *"Attention, Interest, Desire, Action"* and *"Always Be Closing"*. It's a moment of pure cinematic tension, but its aggressive, high-pressure tactics couldn't be further from the reality of modern B2B sales.

True success in closing isn't about manipulation or pushing a customer into a forced decision. It's about fostering trust, solving problems and aligning your solution with the customer's objectives. When done well, closing doesn't feel like a "moment" at all, it feels like a natural progression of a constructive conversation.

In this chapter, I'll explore the art of closing as a journey, not a single event. With the right approach, it doesn't just lead to a signed contract, it lays the foundation for long-term success for both you and your customer.

The four foundations of successful closing

A successful close isn't achieved by chance. It's the result of careful planning, genuine connections and a deep understanding of your customer's objectives and priorities. These four foundational principles will ensure your closing efforts are effective and collaborative.

1. Build trust from the start

The seeds of a successful close are planted in your very first interaction with the customer. Trust isn't something you can ask for, it's earned through transparency, consistency and a genuine focus on solving the customer's challenges.

Building trust means delivering on your promises, no matter how small. It's about being honest, even when the truth might not favour you. When trust is established early, the close feels like a natural continuation of the relationship, not a sudden request for commitment.

2. Address objections as they arise

Unresolved concerns are like potholes on the road to closing, they can derail even the most promising deals. That's why it's essential to unearth and address objections throughout the sales process.

Whether the issue is price, fit, timing or anything else, acknowledging concerns head-on shows respect for the customer's perspective (remember the APAC process we covered in Chapter 16). This approach gives you the opportunity to resolve doubts before they become roadblocks. The fewer objections left unaddressed, the smoother the path to closing will be.

3. Understand their decision-making process

Every customer has a unique way of making decisions. Some rely on detailed data, others on gut instinct, and many involve a team of recommenders, users and gatekeepers. By uncovering how decisions are made in your customer's organisation, you can align your approach to fit their process. Ask questions like:

- "Who else will be involved in this decision?"
- "What steps do you typically follow when choosing a solution like this?"

Understanding their timeline and criteria ensures your closing efforts are timely and aligned. It also positions you as a partner who respects their internal processes.

4. Deploy emotional intelligence

Closing isn't just a logical process, it's an emotional one. Emotional intelligence, the ability to recognise and manage emotions in yourself and others, is a critical asset in successful closing.

Salespeople with high emotional intelligence can read the room, pick up on subtle cues and adapt their tone and communication to match the customer's state of mind. For example, if a stakeholder seems hesitant, an empathetic approach might involve asking open-ended questions to explore their concerns rather than pushing forward too quickly.

Empathy, a cornerstone of emotional intelligence, allows you to genuinely understand your customer's challenges and motivations. It helps you connect on a deeper level, showing that you're not just trying to sell but are invested in your and theirs combined success.

Finally, emotional intelligence helps you stay composed during challenging moments, whether it's a delay in decision-making or an objection that feels personal (something I can remember struggling with from time-to-time). This self-regulation builds trust and keeps the relationship intact, even if the deal doesn't close immediately.

When you use your emotional intelligence, you elevate the entire sales process, transforming closing into a collaboration where you and your customer both feel valued and understood.

By focusing on these four foundations, trust, objection handling, understanding decision-making, and emotional intelligence, you'll create the conditions for closing to feel effortless. It won't be about *"getting the deal"* but about building a partnership where both sides win.

Recognising the right time to close

Timing is everything in closing. Push too early, and you risk alienating the customer. Wait too long and you might miss the opportunity altogether. Recognising the right moment requires a blend of observation, intuition, and preparation.

Key indicators that it's time to close

1. Verbal cues: Listen carefully to what the customer is saying. Statements like "this looks like a good fit" or "how soon could we start"? often indicate readiness to move forward. Questions about implementation, pricing details, or logistics are strong signals that they're envisioning your solution in action
2. Non-verbal cues: Pay attention to body language. Positive signs might include leaning forward, sustained eye contact, or nodding in agreement. Conversely, crossed arms or distracted behaviour may indicate hesitation or unresolved concerns.
3. Behavioural cues: Observe changes in engagement. increased responsiveness, such as replying to emails faster, involving other decision-makers or requesting additional details, shows growing commitment to the decision.
4. Alignment with their timeline: If the customer's decision-making timeline matches your discussions, it's a strong indication they're ready to commit. For instance, if they've mentioned needing a solution by a specific date and you've addressed how you can deliver within that timeframe, it's time to ask for the order.

How to avoid missing the moment

- Stay alert: Always listen for buying signals, both explicit and subtle, throughout the conversation. Missing a cue could delay the process or create uncertainty in the customer's mind.
- Check in regularly: Use trial closes to gauge their readiness without pressuring. Questions like "How does this align with your ideal solution?" or "Are there any other considerations we need to address?" can reveal their position.
- Address concerns early: If objections or doubts surface, tackle them head-on rather than leaving them to fester. Unresolved concerns can delay or derail the closing process.

Balancing confidence and patience

Effective timing is about striking the right balance between confidence and patience. While it's crucial to act when the moment is right, it's equally important to ensure the customer feels in control. A confident, well-prepared salesperson understands that closing is less about forcing a decision and more about guiding the customer to take the next step at the right time.

When you master the art of timing, closing becomes less about chance and more about a smooth process. It's not just about recognising the signals, it's about acting on them with precision and poise.

The AIDA framework: A roadmap to closing

Closing a sale isn't an isolated event, it's the culmination of a journey that moves the customer from awareness to action. The AIDA framework provides a clear roadmap for this process, helping you guide prospects through each stage effectively.

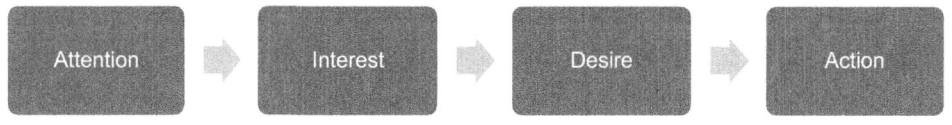

Attention

- Your first task is to capture the customer's attention. Whether it's through a compelling pitch, a well-researched question or an insight that challenges their perspective, this stage is all about making them pause and listen.

- Ask questions like, "did you know that 40% of companies in your sector are losing revenue due to inefficiencies in sales capability?"

Interest

- Once you have their attention, you need to build interest by addressing their pain points or priorities. Highlight how your solution can help, using data, case studies, or success stories.
- Ask open-ended questions to encourage engagement and uncover deeper insights into their needs.

Desire

- Interest turns into desire when the customer begins to see the value of your solution for their specific challenges. This is where emotional intelligence plays a vital role, empathising with their goals and reinforcing the benefits they care about most.
- As questions like, "Imagine cutting your downtime by 30%, how much would that impact your bottom line?"

Action

- The final step is guiding the customer toward action, whether it's scheduling a demo, signing a contract or agreeing to next steps. Here, your closing techniques come into play, making it easy and logical for them to say "yes".
- Ensure the customer feels confident by addressing any remaining objections and providing a clear path forward.

Why AIDA works

The AIDA framework ensures that your efforts are aligned with the customer's journey. By addressing their needs at each stage, you're not just selling; you're creating a seamless experience that builds trust and momentum toward the close.

Adapting to different customer personalities

As we have previously discussed, no two customers are the same, and understanding their unique personalities can be the key to closing the deal effectively. Tailoring your approach based on a customer's preferences and decision-making style helps you build rapport, address their concerns and present solutions in ways that resonate with them.

Four common buyer types and how to adapt

1. The analytical buyer

   - Traits: Data-driven, detail-oriented, and cautious. They value facts, figures and logical reasoning.
   - How to close: Provide clear data and evidence to support your claims. Be prepared to answer detailed questions and avoid pushing for a quick decision.
   - Example: "Based on the ROI projections we discussed, how do you feel this solution fits your business case?"
   - DISC type mapping: C (Conscientiousness), focused on accuracy, quality and logical analysis.

2. The results-oriented buyer

   - Traits: Fast-paced, decisive and focused on achieving results. They appreciate efficiency and clear outcomes.
   - How to close: Be concise and action oriented. Highlight the direct benefits of your solution and provide a clear and direct path forward.
   - Example: "\this will solve the issue within the first quarter. Can we move forward today?"
   - DISC type mapping: D (Dominance), driven by goals, results, and decisiveness.

3. The relationship-focused buyer

   - Traits: Values trust, connection and long-term partnerships. They make decisions based on rapport and alignment with their goals.
   - How to close: Focus on collaboration and mutual benefit. Emphasise your commitment to your joint success and reassure them of your ongoing support.
   - Example: "With this partnership, we'll work closely to ensure these goals are achieved. Shall we get started together?"
   - DISC type mapping: S (Steadiness), prioritises relationships, stability, and mutual trust.

4. The Risk-Averse Buyer

   - Traits: Hesitant and focused on avoiding potential pitfalls. They want reassurance and minimal risk.

- How to close: Provide guarantees, case studies or references to mitigate perceived risks. Break down the decision into manageable steps.
- Example: "To ensure this works for you, let's start with a pilot phase and evaluate the results. Does that feel comfortable for you?"
- DISC type mapping: I (Influence), while hesitant, they value guidance and examples that inspire confidence.

Why it all matters

Adapting to different customer personalities shows that you understand their priorities and decision-making styles. It builds trust, reduces friction and ensures that your closing approach feels tailored, not templated. Mapping these personalities to the DISC model provides additional clarity on how to approach each type effectively. By understanding these traits, you'll create a stronger connection and increase the likelihood of a successful close.

Closing techniques for the modern salesperson

While closing shouldn't feel like a "technique," there are ways that can help guide the conversation toward a commitment. Here are a few approaches that work in today's B2B environment.

1. The assumptive close

This method assumes the customer is ready to move forward and focuses on next steps. Example: "Shall we schedule the onboarding session for next week or does the week after work better for your team?" This approach works best when the customer has shown strong buying signals.

2. The summary close

Recap the key points you've discussed, tying your solution directly to their needs. Example: "You mentioned that reducing downtime and improving efficiency are top priorities. With our solution, you'll see a 30% reduction in downtime within the first quarter. Shall we move forward?" This technique reinforces the value you're offering while making it easy for the customer to say yes.

3. The alternative close

Give the customer two options, both leading to a decision. Example: "Would you prefer the standard package, or should we start with the premium option to maximise results?" This subtly shifts the focus from if they'll buy to how they'll buy.

4. The trial close

Test the waters to gauge their readiness before fully committing to the close. Example: "How does this solution align with your team's objectives?" If they respond positively, you can move confidently to the final close.

5. Simply ask for the order

Sometimes, the most effective strategy is also the simplest: just ask. Once you've presented your case, addressed objections and confirmed interest, say, "Would you like to move forward?" or "When would you like to place your order?" It's straightforward, eliminates ambiguity and often works because it avoids overcomplicating the close. Customers appreciate clarity and decisiveness, especially D and C type personalities. This approach is the one I use most often and is my personal favourite.

Practical tips for closing

1. Be confident

Confidence is contagious. If you hesitate or seem unsure, the customer will pick up on it and may second-guess their decision. Approach the close with certainty in the value you're offering.

2. Stay customer-centric

Always frame the close in terms of the customer's goals. For example: "By moving forward today, we can ensure your team is fully operational by the start of the next quarter."

3. Use silence strategically

Once you've asked for the business, stop talking. Silence creates space for the customer to process and respond. Many salespeople feel the urge to fill the gap. Resist it and let them take their time.

4. Prepare for the close

Before entering the closing conversation, review:

- The customer's key objectives.
- Any unresolved objections and how you've addressed them.
- The steps required to finalise the deal.

The power of follow-up post-close

Closing the deal isn't the end of your sales process, it's the beginning of delivering value. A thoughtful follow-up after the close ensures that your customer feels confident in their decision and sets the stage for a lasting partnership.

Why follow-up matters

- It reinforces confidence: Even after agreeing to move forward, customers can experience buyer's remorse. A proactive follow-up to thank them and reiterate how your solution aligns with their goals can ease any lingering doubts.
- It demonstrates professionalism: Following through on your promises, such as sending next steps, contracts, or timelines, all reinforces your reliability and credibility.
- It lays the groundwork for success: Follow-up conversations are an opportunity to ensure a smooth onboarding process and align expectations for delivery.

How to follow up effectively

1. Send a personalised thank you: A genuine thank you email or a hand-written note (which has a fantastic impact, these days) or phone call goes a long way in making the customer feel valued. Mention specific aspects of your discussions to show you were truly engaged.

2. Provide a clear next steps plan: Outline what happens next: timelines, deliverables and points of contact. Customers appreciate clarity and structure after deciding.

3. Check in regularly: Keep in touch during implementation to ensure they're happy with the progress. Regular updates demonstrate your continued commitment and provide opportunities to address any concerns.

The role of follow-up in future opportunities

A great follow-up isn't just about the deal at hand, it's also an investment in your future. A customer who feels supported and valued is more likely to become a repeat client, refer you to others or provide glowing testimonials.

Remember, your relationship with the customer starts with the close, but it doesn't end there. By following up effectively, you'll turn a successful sale into the foundation for ongoing success and future up-sell and cross-sell opportunities (which we will cover in the next chapter).

Closing with purpose

As we've explored throughout this chapter, closing isn't about flashy gimmicks or high-pressure tactics; it's about preparation, trust and collaboration. The key to successful closing lies in consistently aligning your solution with the customer's objectives, priorities and guiding them toward a decision that feels right for them, not forced upon them.

When you approach closing as a natural extension of the sales process, it becomes effortless. Every question you've asked, every objection you've addressed and every value you've reinforced since your first meeting with the customer, paves the way for a confident "yes." This isn't selling, it's solving problems and challenges; helping your customer take the next step towards success and making you someone easy to buy from.

A 30-minute exercise to improve your closing

Over the years, I've used a 30-minute interactive role-playing exercise with the sales teams I've led to help them refine their closing techniques. This exercise simulates real world scenarios, focusing on recognising buying signals, adapting to different customer personalities and applying effective closing methods.

Objective

To practice and improve closing skills by engaging in role-playing scenarios that simulate common challenges for B2B salespeople.

What you'll need

- A list of prepared sales scenarios (I've provided examples below).
- Role cards for different customer personalities (analytical, relationship-focused, results-oriented, risk-averse).

- Stopwatch or timer.
- A notepad for participants to jot down feedback.

Timing and structure (30 minutes)

Introduction (5 minutes)

- Trainer's brief: Explain the objective of the exercise. Have participants read this chapter before the exercise; then remind them of the importance of identifying customer buying signals, choosing the right closing techniques and tailoring approaches to customer personalities.

Key skills to practice

- Recognising verbal, non-verbal and behavioural cues
- Selecting the appropriate closing technique (Assumptive, Summary, Trial etc)
- Adapting communication to suit different customer types.

Role-playing scenarios (20 minutes)

Step 1: Split participants into pairs or small groups.

- One person acts as the salesperson
- The other(s) act as the customer, adopting a specific personality type (analytical, relationship-focused, results-oriented, risk-averse).

Step 2: Assign each group a scenario. Some examples could be:

- Scenario 1: The customer is hesitant due to pricing concerns (risk-averse).
- Scenario 2: The customer needs detailed ROI projections (analytical).
- Scenario 3: The customer is eager but undecided between two package options (results-oriented).
- Scenario 4: The customer is highly focused on building a long-term partnership (relationship-focused).

Step 3: The salesperson has five minutes to engage the customer, recognise the buying signals, address objections and use a closing technique.

Debrief and feedback (5 minutes)

After each round, the person playing the role of the customer provides constructive feedback.

- Did the salesperson recognize their signals and address concerns?
- Was the chosen closing technique appropriate?
- How could they improve communication skills?

This exercise will provide a hands-on, interactive experience enabling you to recognise cues, select effective closing techniques and tailor your approach to different customer types.

A closing story: A trip to the theatre

In 2017, I had the pleasure of visiting the Playhouse Theatre in London to see a production of *Glengarry Glen Ross* with my business partner, David Breen. As longtime fans of the film, we were eager to experience the sharp dialogue and high-stakes drama live on stage. Naturally, I was especially excited to witness Alec Baldwin's iconic "Always Be Closing" speech performed in person and looked forward to saying his infamous dialogue in unison with him.

As the play unfolded, I found myself waiting and waiting for that moment. Intermission came and went (which included a very nice glass of Merlot if I remember correctly), yet still no sign of Baldwin's character or his blistering pep talk. By the end of the show, it finally dawned on me: Baldwin's character didn't exist in the play.

That unforgettable scene, so deeply embedded in popular culture, was a Hollywood invention. David, of course, knew this all along but had chosen not to tell me, relishing my growing confusion throughout the evening (in a nice way).

While I couldn't help but laugh at the revelation, it also reminded me of an important lesson for sales and life: always set clear expectations. Just as I had assumed every production of *Glengarry Glen Ross* included Baldwin's infamous speech, it's easy to assume our customers share our knowledge, values or priorities. In reality, they don't always know or care about our "ABC", they care about solving the challenges.

Great salespeople, like great storytellers, adapt their approach to their audience. They clarify what to expect, ensure alignment, and avoid leaving anyone waiting for something that was never part of the deal. After all, closing isn't about theatrics or assumptions, it's about connection, collaboration and delivering on what matters most to them.

.

Chapter 19: Upselling and cross-selling

"Success is a journey, not a destination. It requires constant effort, vigilance and re-evaluation." — Mark Twain.

In my personal experience, closing the sale is always a significant milestone, but if you're clever, it's far from the end of the journey. When a customer commits to a purchase, you're opening the door to an incredible opportunity; the chance to strengthen your relationship with them through upselling and cross-selling.

This isn't just about increasing your revenue; it's about showing your customers you truly understand their needs and can deliver even greater value to them. In this chapter, I'll walk you through the techniques and best practices I've found most effective for integrating upselling and cross-selling into your sales approach.

Understanding upselling and cross-selling

Before going any further, let's clarify the distinction.

- **Upselling** is encouraging your customer to purchase a more premium or enhanced version of the product or service they are buying (or have bought). For example, upgrading a customer from a standard subscription to a premium plan with additional features.
- **Cross-selling** is recommending complementary products or services that enhance the customer's initial purchase. For instance, suggesting a protective case or extended warranty for a new smartphone.

I've provided a simple definition and example of each scenario below.

Upselling might involve:

- An increase in a business insurance policy from £200k to £500k with a more comprehensive cover package.
- An increase in a data circuit speed from 1 Gig to 10 Gig.
- Moving a customer from a MacBook Pro 13' (128GB) at £1,499 to MacBook Pro 13" (256 GB) at £1,599.

Cross-selling might involve

- Selling a building insurance policy to an existing legal insurance customer.
- Adding a unified voice communication system to an existing data circuit customer.
- Adding a carry case, extra power plug and headphones to use with a MacBook and extended insurance cover for it

Both techniques focus on delivering additional value to the customer while maximising the sales potential for your business.

Why upselling and cross-selling matters

In B2B sales, leveraging upselling and cross-selling opportunities is pivotal to developing long-term mutually beneficial partnerships with your customers. It not only increases the value you derive from existing customer relationships but also contributes significantly to your company's bottom line. Here's a list of key benefits that you get from doing it successfully.

- Increased revenue: It can significantly boost the average transaction value, driving higher profitability without the need to acquire new customers.
- Cost efficiency: Selling to existing customers is five to 25 times more cost-effective than acquiring new ones.
- Higher likelihood of success: Existing customers are up to 70% more likely to purchase compared to new ones (subject to you doing a good job).
- Lifecycle flexibility: It can be applied at any stage of the customer lifecycle, fostering a proactive relationship.
- Enhanced customer experience: By tailoring additional offers to meet your customer needs, you position your yourself as a trusted advisor rather than a mere salesperson.
- Customer retention: It provides a more comprehensive solution, encourages loyalty, reducing churn and fostering long-term relationships. A five percent increase in customer retention can boost profits by 25% to 95% (Frederick Reichheld, Bain & Co.).

Ultimately, upselling and cross-selling transforms how you engage with your customers. It leads to lead to sustained growth, reduced costs, and heightened customer satisfaction.

Techniques for upselling and cross-selling

The techniques I'll cover not only provide customers with better options but also enhance the overall sales experience. As highlighted in earlier chapters, you make yourself someone who is "*easy to buy from*".

Upselling techniques

- Highlight benefits, not features: Emphasise how the premium option will solve problems more effectively, save time or provide additional convenience. Example: "Our premium package includes 24/7 customer support and advanced analytics, ensuring you're always ahead of your competition."
- Use social proof: Share testimonials and case studies from customers who benefited from the upgraded option: Example: "After upgrading to our premium service, XYZ Corporation saw a 30% increase in efficiency and a 20% reduction in operational costs. Here's what their CEO had to say: "*The premium service has been a game-changer for us. The advanced features and dedicated support have significantly streamlined our processes and improved our overall performance.*"
- Offer limited-time incentives: Encourage upgrades by providing discounts or additional features for a limited time. Example: "If you upgrade to Pro within the next 24 hours, we'll include a free setup consultation."
- Present it as the default option: Position the premium offering as the most popular or standard choice. This subtle framing can influence decision-making. Example: "Our Premium Plan is our most popular choice, selected by 70% of our customers."
- Highlight cost savings: Show how the premium option can save money in the long run through efficiencies or bundled services. Example: "By switching to our premium subscription, you can save up to 15% on annual costs compared to monthly payments. Additionally, our premium plan includes bundled services such as free software updates and extended warranty, which can save you an additional £500 per year."

Cross-selling techniques

- Bundle products: Create value-packed bundles that combine the main product with complementary items at a discounted rate. Example: "Get a free set of accessories when you purchase this camera."
- Utilise recommendations: Use phrases like "Customers who bought this also purchased…" or "Based on your initial purchase, you might find this useful."
- Use visual cues: Display images or diagrams showing how complementary products work together to create a complete solution.
- Follow-up offers: Reach out post-purchase with targeted offers for add-ons or services based on the customer's initial choice.
- Incentivise referrals: Offer discounts or bonuses for customers who refer other products or services to peers or colleagues.

By implementing these techniques, you can significantly enhance your sales results.

Avoiding common pitfalls

When it comes to upselling and cross-selling, even well-intentioned approaches can backfire without careful execution. To avoid common pitfalls, consider the following:

- Poor timing: Avoid attempting to upsell or cross-sell when a customer is experiencing issues or dissatisfaction. Address their concerns first and only present additional offers when the relationship is stable and positive.
- Overloading the customer: Bombarding the customer with too many options can lead to decision fatigue. Limit your suggestions to one or two highly relevant choices. Take your time and target the offer you genuinely believe will benefit the customer most.
- Forgetting the relationship: Never prioritise the sale over the customer's trust. A short-term gain isn't worth risking the potential for a long-term, mutually beneficial partnership.
- Not knowing your stuff: Ensure you are well-versed in the features, benefits and potential downsides of every upsell and cross-sell opportunity. Confidence and product knowledge build trust and lead to more effective sales conversations.
- Misjudging customer needs: Avoid making assumptions about what the customer values. Take the time to listen carefully and ask thoughtful questions to ensure your recommendations align with their goals.

By recognising these potential pitfalls, you can refine your approach to create a seamless and positive experience for your customers. The key is maintaining balance and focusing on adding value without overwhelming or alienating the customer.

Measuring success

To gauge the effectiveness of your upselling and cross-selling efforts, track your performance by recording:

- Average order value (AOV): Monitor changes in the average transaction size.
- Conversion rates: Measure how often upsell and cross-sell recommendations result in additional purchases.
- Customer feedback: Regularly solicit feedback to ensure your strategies are perceived as helpful rather than intrusive.

Mastering the art of upselling and cross-selling requires a delicate balance of timing and customer focus. When done right it not only drives revenue, but also strengthens customer relationships by delivering enhanced value. By integrating these practices into your sales process, you can create win-win scenarios where both you and your customers benefit.

Chapter 20: Developing your skill set

"An investment in knowledge always pays the best interest." - Benjamin Franklin

One of the most striking lessons I've learned in my career is that success in sales is not static; it's a journey of continuous growth.

I once met a salesperson who confidently proclaimed they had 20 years of experience in sales." However, as I observed their approach, it became clear that what they really had was one year of experience, which they had repeated 19 times.

They hadn't evolved, adapted or sought to improve. They relied on the same strategies and methods they learned in their first year, as their industry and their customers changed around them.

That individual's career stalled because they didn't recognise the importance of developing their skill set.

This chapter is about avoiding that fate. In B2B sales, your skills are your currency, and it's up to you, not your employer or your manager, to ensure you're continually improving your craft.

Why skills development is your responsibility

In sales, no one has more to gain from your success or to lose from your failure than you. While companies may provide training and resources, the responsibility for your growth ultimately lies with you. Taking ownership of your skill set means:

- Staying relevant: Industries evolve, customer expectations shift and new tools emerge. To stay competitive, you must adapt.
- Seizing opportunities: Career advancement, larger accounts, and higher earnings come to those who continually improve their capabilities.
- Building confidence: The more skilled you are, the more confident you'll feel tackling challenges and pursuing ambitious goals.
- Setting yourself apart: In a field where everyone is chasing the same opportunities, being better than your competition is essential.

Neglecting skill development, on the other hand, is a recipe for stagnation. The moment you think you've "arrived" or that you know it all, is the moment your career begins to plateau.

Ways to develop your skill set

There are countless ways to improve as a salesperson. The most successful individuals take a multi-faceted approach, combining formal education with self-directed learning and on-the-job experience. Here (in my opinion) are some of the most effective methods.

1. Attend sales training programs

Invest in high-quality sales training courses, whether offered by your company or through external providers. These programs often cover topics like negotiation, objection handling and prospecting in depth.

Don't just attend the course, apply what you learn. Choose one or two techniques to implement immediately and track the results

2. Learn from your peers

Colleagues and mentors can be incredible sources of wisdom. I have been fortunate enough to work with and for some great people who have contributed to building my skill set over the years.

Observe how top-performing salespeople handle customer interactions, and don't be afraid to ask questions. If, for example, a colleague is particularly skilled at closing deals, ask them about their approach and how they handle objections. But resist the temptation to compare yourself to others negatively. Focus on learning, not competing.

3. Use online resources

The internet is a treasure trove of learning opportunities, from webinars and podcasts to articles and video tutorials. Platforms like LinkedIn Learning, Coursera, and YouTube offer content tailored to sales professionals.

Dedicate 30 minutes a week to exploring a new topic or skill through online resources

4. Practice, practice, practice

Theoretical knowledge is valuable, but real growth happens through application. Role-playing scenarios with colleagues, practicing presentations and rehearsing meetings are excellent ways to refine your techniques.

Record yourself during role-play exercises or video calls and review the footage to identify areas for improvement.

5. Read sales and business books

The fact that you're here means you have already latched onto this one. Books by industry experts can provide new perspectives and strategies. Read when you can and share your key takeaways with your colleagues

5. Never think you know it all

One of the biggest obstacles to growth is complacency. When salespeople believe they've mastered everything they need to know, they close themselves off to new ideas and opportunities for improvement. The beginning of wisdom lies in the admission of ignorance.

Developing your skill set is not just a professional responsibility, it's a personal commitment. In B2B sales, the landscape is too competitive, and the stakes are too high to rely on outdated methods or to assume that you've learned everything there is to know.

By taking ownership of your growth, seeking out learning opportunities, and remaining humble enough to recognise areas for improvement, you'll set yourself apart as a top performer. Remember, the process of the sale is a journey, not a destination. The more you invest in your skills, the more successful and fulfilling your career will be.

Don't be the person with one year of experience repeated 19 times. Be the salesperson who grows, evolves, and consistently delivers value. Your customers, colleagues, and future self will all thank you.

Chapter 21: Pulling it all together: the best version of you

At the heart of a successful career in B2B sales lies the ability to combine an array of skills, disciplines and attributes into a cohesive whole.

The best salespeople don't simply master one area; they integrate the art and science of selling to become the best version of themselves. In my experience, there are three key attributes that define the most successful sales professionals: **emotional intelligence, intellectual horsepower, and work ethic.**

In this chapter I'll pull together the threads from everything we've discussed so far - qualification, building relationships, understanding personality types, negotiation - and weave them into these three fundamental attributes. By focusing on developing these qualities, you **can** position yourself for consistent success.

1. Emotional intelligence: the foundation of connection

Emotional intelligence is the ability to understand and manage your emotions while effectively responding to the emotions of others. In sales, where relationships drive results, it is the cornerstone of success.

The role of emotional intelligence in sales:

- Building trust and rapport: Customers buy from people they trust. Emotional intelligence helps you build genuine connections by empathising with your customers' challenges and showing you truly understand their needs.
- Navigating challenges: Whether handling objections, negotiating terms or addressing concerns, emotional intelligence allows you to remain calm and professional, even under pressure.
- Adapting to personality types: As we explored earlier, different customers have different communication styles and preferences. Emotional intelligence helps you read the room, tailor your approach, and connect with diverse personalities.

Practical Applications

- Active listening: Asking intelligent questions is crucial but so is listening to the answers. Pay attention not just to what your customers say but how they say it. Tone, body language, and non-verbal cues provide valuable insights.

- Empathy in action: When a customer expresses frustration or concern, validate their feelings before offering a solution. For example, "I understand that this is a significant investment for your team. Let's explore how we can maximise the return for you."
- Staying resilient: Sales can be full of rejection and setbacks. Emotional intelligence helps you bounce back from disappointments, maintaining your focus and optimism.

2. Intellectual horsepower: thinking two steps ahead

Intellectual horsepower isn't just about raw intelligence; it's about applying strategic thinking, problem-solving and adaptability to every situation. B2B sales is complex, and success requires a sharp mind capable of understanding intricate customer needs, identifying opportunities, and crafting tailored solutions.

The role of intellectual horsepower in sales

- Strategic qualification: Knowing which opportunities to pursue and which to walk away from is a skill rooted in intellectual horsepower. It's about analysing data, asking the right questions, and making informed decisions.
- Solving problems: Customers aren't just buying products or services. They're buying solutions to their problems. Intellectual horsepower allows you to diagnose issues, propose innovative solutions, and articulate the value of your offering.
- As each year goes by, customers become even more well informed. To add value they expect you to be an expert authority on your product or service. Intellectual horsepower enables you to master the details, answer tough questions, and confidently demonstrate how your offering meets their needs.

Practical applications

- Mastering your industry: Knowledge is power. Stay informed about industry trends, competitor activity, and your customers' markets. The more you know, the more value you can bring to the table.
- Product expertise: Be the go-to expert on your product or service. Understand its features, benefits, limitations, and unique value propositions. Customers respect and trust salespeople who know their offerings inside out.
- Planning ahead: Whether it's a pipeline forecast or a sales meeting, success comes from preparation. As we discussed in earlier chapters, knowing what you want to achieve and how you'll achieve it is critical.

3. Work ethic: the engine that drives results

The final piece of the puzzle is work ethic. In sales, talent and intelligence are only part of the equation. Consistent effort, discipline and perseverance are what separate the good from the great.

The role of work ethic in sales:

- Consistent prospecting: As we explored in the chapter on prospecting, filling your pipeline is a non-negotiable task. A strong work ethic ensures you dedicate time every day to prospecting, even when it's uncomfortable.
- Follow-through: The best salespeople do what they say they'll do, when they say they'll do it. They follow up on commitments, meet deadlines and exceed expectations, building trust and credibility with every interaction.
- Continuous improvement: Sales is a field where you never stop learning. A strong work ethic drives you to seek feedback, refine your skills, and push yourself to new heights.

Practical applications

- Daily discipline: Start each day with a clear plan of what you want to achieve. Prioritise high-value activities, like customer meetings, prospecting, and pipeline management.
- Going the extra mile: Whether it's preparing a detailed proposal or rehearsing your presentation, small efforts add up to big results.
- Staying consistent: Work ethic isn't about occasional bursts of effort - it's about showing up and delivering every single day. It's also about recognising that you can't work 24/7, so work smart and then stop. Rest and recovery are vital aspects to a vigorous professional life.

Weaving it all together

The best salespeople I have worked with combine emotional intelligence, intellectual horsepower, and work ethic into a seamless whole. These attributes aren't independent; they feed into and reinforce one another.

- **Emotional intelligence enables collaboration**: Emotional intelligence helps you work effectively with colleagues and customers, tapping into the power of teamwork and shared expertise.

- **Intellectual horsepower drives expertise**: A sharp mind allows you to adapt, innovate, and position yourself as a trusted authority in your field.
- **Work ethic enables execution**: All the emotional intelligence and intellectual horsepower in the world won't help if you don't put in the effort to apply them consistently.

Becoming the best version of yourself

To pull it all together, consider this: success in B2B sales isn't about mastering one skill or closing one deal, it's about becoming the best version of yourself, every day. Here are some actionable steps to get there:

1. **Set clear goals**: Know what success looks like for you, whether it's achieving your sales target, earning a promotion, or building stronger customer relationships.
2. **Invest in yourself**: Read, learn, and seek feedback constantly. Invest in yourself for the biggest return.
3. **Balance the art and science**: Combine the art of relationship-building with the science of data-driven decision-making and robust processes.
4. **Stay true to your values**: Integrity is non-negotiable. Be authentic, honest, and customer-focused.
5. **Celebrate the wins**: Success is a journey, not a destination. Take time to acknowledge your achievements and learn from your challenges.

Your numbers shall set you free

At the end of the day, selling is a performance-driven profession. Embracing everything we've covered in this book will hopefully improve your ability to achieve consistent results, exceed your targets and unlock the opportunities and rewards that come with success.

Becoming the best version of yourself isn't a one-time effort, it's a career journey. The skills and attributes we've explored in this book are your roadmap. Use them, refine them, and build a career that reflects your full potential. Because when you bring together the art and science of B2B sales, you will not only hit your numbers, you will find that they set you free.

Printed in Great Britain
by Amazon